How to Read

THE CONSTITUTION

The Declaration of Independence

How to Read

THE CONSTITUTION

The Declaration of Independence

PAUL B. SKOUSEN

PUBLISHER
SALT LAKE CITY, UT

Izzard Ink Publishing Company
PO Box 522251
Salt Lake City, Utah 84152
www.izzardink.com

LIBRARY OF CONGRESS CONTROL NUMBER: 2016943259
Designed by Alissa Rose Theodor

First edition July 4, 2016
Second edition July 4, 2017

www.paulskousen.com
Contact the author at info@paulskousen.com

Softback ISBN: 978-1-53485-375-1
Hardback ISBN: 978-1-63072-108-4
eBook ISBN: 978-1-63072-109-1
Interactive eBook ISBN: 978-1-63072-110-7

Thomas Jefferson

September 28, 1820

"I know no safe depository of the ultimate powers of the society, but the people themselves: and if we think them not enlightened enough to exercise their control with a wholesome discretion, the remedy is, not to take it from them, but to inform their discretion by education. This is the true corrective of abuses of constitutional power."

PREFACE

The Constitution is not difficult to read when you know what to look for. Knowing the purpose and intent of each Article, and using a glossary to clarify its words and terms, makes understanding come faster.

The Declaration of Independence may seem abstract and difficult at first, but gently taking it apart to look at its details shows it to be one of the most powerful and insightful political statements in history.

Putting America's two founding documents together makes their 225-year-old message shine as modern, as important, as revealing, and as relevant today as they were when they were first written more than two centuries ago.

This guide is for anyone who wants to know the essence of the Constitution and the Declaration of Independence.

It is for the newly arrived immigrants to the United States who wonder about the grand vista of their new liberties.

It is for the student just learning about America's founding documents for the first time.

It is for the politician who needs a quick refresher on the powers and limitations of government.

It is for the individual trying to understand how to protect the human rights of people around the world.

It is for those who want to become familiar with the Constitution and Declaration but don't have the necessary time to do more than just read them.

Learning to better understand these two documents will recast them from antiquated reflections of an earlier time into brilliant guideposts that point the way through the highs and the lows, the successes and losses, the prosperity and the challenges of managing the most amazing freedom formula ever invented.

CONTENTS

CONTENTS

PART I

START AT THE BEGINNING

WHY READ THE CONSTITUTION?

How do millions of people live together without tearing each other apart to acquire food, shelter and power? Fighting for survival has been a terrible problem that started with the beginning of human history. It took us thousands of years to finally find a peaceful solution, and when we did, an astonishing thing happened. A totally new kind of nation arose that changed the course of history. The fighting stopped, order was restored, and the people started living together in peace and prosperity. What changed?

The U.S. Constitution was that change. It was the brilliant, ingenious and elegant solution that humanity had been missing. It pointed the human race toward self-government as the best solution to preserve human rights and to encourage inventive exploration.

With just 4,379 words, the men who framed the Constitution helped *We the People* form a more perfect union, establish justice, ensure domestic tranquility, promote our general welfare, and secure the blessings of liberty to ourselves and to our posterity.

For those who were there, this new way to govern came as nothing short of an amazing miracle.

By the People and For the People

The Framers wrote the Constitution so it was easy to read, easy to understand and easy to apply. They reasoned that if the law was basic and simple the people could keep track of the power they gave to their leaders and watch for abuses.

The final version of the Constitution was completed on September 17, 1787. It gave a clean statement of purposes with a well-engineered plan to achieve them. It is not complicated. It has order, structure, and simple principles that everyone can understand. It is a practical guide that helps us navigate through this nation's most perplexing problems.

The Promise

The Constitution requires two actions from the citizens it protects: First, honest obedience to its rules and framework; and second, reading it often.

Reading the Constitution produces an amazing outcome. Americans discover for themselves the limits that are placed on their leaders. With such knowledge they are better able to compel over-zealous politicians into restraint and fairness so their natural rights are safe from abuse and destruction.

We read the Constitution, therefore, to stay free.

WHAT DOES IT DO?

The Constitution created three branches of government to run the country. Each branch has specific assignments which the other branches are forbidden to touch. All their duties are spelled out in writing so that everyone knows what the branches *must* do, what they *may* do, and what they *can't* do. If there is a job to be done and it's not on anyone's official list, that job falls to the individual states or to the people themselves.

The Constitution and the Rule of Law

Government is defined in the dictionary as "a system of ruling or controlling." Most people view their government as a political party such as democrat, republican, socialist, independent, labor party, etc. However, those names don't tell us very much about their plans for "ruling or controlling." That's why the American Framers measured the world's political systems according to how much power and political force they exercised over their people.

In other words, the measuring stick is not political parties but political power.

Using that measuring stick the Framers discovered that almost all political systems fall into one of two extremes: anarchy or tyranny.

The Problem of Anarchy and Tyranny

Anarchy is chaos. It's a system where there is no law, no government, no control, and no central political power. Those systems allow mobs to form, to impose their will on others, and to take as they please. Stealing and fighting is normal, and there is no safety for anyone.

Tyranny is at the opposite extreme with too much power, too much control, and too much government. Whatever the ruler commands, the people are forced to obey. This is called Ruler's Law.

Finding the Balanced Center

The Framers' goal was to find the right balance between too much political power and none at all.

Their solution is found in the Constitution where the people hold all of the ruling and controlling power. They may delegate and assign certain powers to the government, but always under the watchful care of their representatives. This is called People's Law.

The Framers' view of these three forms of law and government might look like this:

All Power in the People

The contrast between Ruler's Law and People's Law is illustrated below.

In Ruler's Law, all the power is held by the ruler at the top level as shown by the inverted pyramid. The lower units of government are granted fewer powers until, at the bottom, the individual is granted the least power of all.

In People's Law, all the power is in the individual as shown at the base of the upright pyramid. The higher units of government are granted fewer powers until the highest level, the national government, which has the least power of all. The orientation of the pyramids illustrates that Ruler's Law is vulnerable to toppling while People's Law is more stable and harder to disturb.

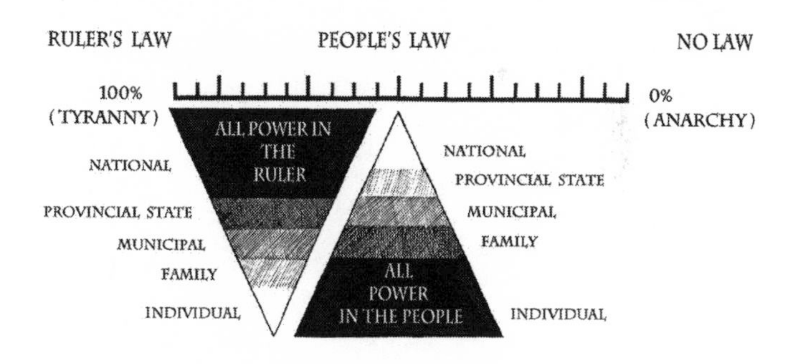

The Only Guarantee

The Constitution's most fundamental purpose is to guarantee the people's right to make responsible choices. The word "responsible" means to respect the same rights in others as you claim for yourself.

Those choices include the freedom to try, to buy, to sell, and to fail. It's a broad landscape of limitless possibilities, all within a framework that gives each person equal rights and protections.

The Constitution cannot, however, guarantee the same opportunities, circumstances, skills, abilities, acceptance, or the same outcome for those choices. It cannot guarantee that your candidate or favorite team will win. It cannot guarantee that your business idea will become a big success. It cannot guarantee a car in every driveway, a chicken in every pot, or a smart phone in every pocket.

In answer to, "What does it do?" the Constitution puts the people in total control of their own government.

WHY DID THEY WRITE IT?

In the 1760s, England's King George III was angry, sick, and struggling. Great Britain had just won a long war with France and the British were deeply in debt. The King and his government sought relief by taxing the American colonies.

The colonists were infuriated because they had no say regarding the new taxes and restrictions. They started writing letters and sending messengers in protest. They created the Continental Association to carry out a trade boycott against Great Britain. It was the first time the 13 colonies formally joined together to exert their rights and resist British authority. The Association was very successful while it lasted and British trade plummeted.

The King ignored these efforts and bore down even harder. The Americans were finally pushed to take drastic action. They saw no way forward to regain their liberties except to revolt and break away from England. The Declaration of Independence was their formal announcement.

The Declaration captures the spirit and ideals of the War for Independence, and shows why the Americans were so frustrated with the King. After they won the war and created their new government, those frustrations were written right into their new Constitution. For each act of oppression the King inflicted upon the colonists there is a constitutional section, clause, or protection to prevent such abuse from ever happening again.

The Declaration explains the "Why?" of the Constitution—its purpose, its mission, and its fulfillment of a great new promise called liberty.

Let's take a brief tour.

PART II

THE DECLARATION OF INDEPENDENCE

EIGHT ANCIENT PRINCIPLES

The Fundamental Ideals of Freedom

In June 1776, Thomas Jefferson was given the difficult task of writing the text for the Declaration of Independence. The Declaration was the formal announcement that the American colonies were breaking from Britain.

It took Jefferson 17 days to write this masterpiece. Most of those days were spent putting into words the ancient principles of liberty that Jefferson had been studying all of his adult life. These words would create the powerful philosophical framework for the Constitution that would be written 11 years later. This is how Jefferson presented those principles of liberty and freedom.

1. Self-Evident Truths.

Sound government should be based on clear and self-evident truths that are so obvious that no one could reasonably question them.

2. Laws are of God and of Nature.

There are laws which all people must obey. Whether the laws come from God or from

Nature, they do exist, and all humans are equally connected to them.

3. All Humans are Equal.

All men and women are equal in their rights, equal before the bar of justice, and equal in God's sight. Even though individual attributes and circumstances will be different for everyone, people are by nature equal in their rights.

4. Rights are Unalienable.

As a law of God and Nature's God, human rights are universal and in every person. They may not be taken away. Other rights that are vested (supplied by the government) may be removed, but not human rights.

5. Life, Liberty, and Property.

Among the most important human rights is the right to life, the right to liberty, and the right to acquire, develop, and sell private property.

6. Governments Must Protect Rights.

The most basic reason for people to organize themselves into a nation is to set up a government that will protect their human rights.

7. Governments Are Permitted to Exist.

The people themselves have the right to decide how they are to be governed and by whom.

Governments have no rights except those granted by the people.

8. People May Change Government At Will.

The people have the right and the duty to replace a government that doesn't protect their human rights.

Along with these eight essential principles came wonderful promises—a free nation, a free people, united and indivisible, founded on liberty and equality. These promises stirred hope for freedom among the three million colonists of 1776. Here is how those promises were initially structured and justified. They called it their Declaration of Independence.

STRUCTURE & CONTENT

How is the Declaration Organized?
The Declaration of Independence has five parts.

1 **Preamble: The Purpose of this Declaration**

This section declares it is the people's natural right to change their governments and act independently according to their own will.

THE DECLARATION OF INDEPENDENCE

Action of Second continental Congress, July 4, 1776

The unanimous Declaration of the thirteen Untied States of America

1 → WHEN in the Course of human Events, it becomes necessary for one People to dissolve the Political Bands which have connected them with another, and to assume among the Powers of the Earth, the separate and equal Station to which the Laws of Nature and of Nature's God entitle them, a decent Respect to Opinions of Mankind requires that they should declare the causes which impel them to the Separation.

2 Assertion: Rights are Unalienable

This paragraph is a summary of the eight immutable (fixed) and self-evident principles of personal human rights and good government.

2 → WE hold these truths to be self-evident, that all men are created equal, that they are endowed by their Creator with certain unalienable Rights, that among these are Life, Liberty and the pursuit of Happiness.–That to secure these rights, Governments are instituted among Men, deriving their just powers from the consent of the governed, –That whenever any Form of Government

3 Charges: What the King Did

This is a list of 27 charges and grievances against King George III and his government, the proof that those people were enemies to freedom.

He has refused his Assent to Laws, the most wholesome and necessary for the public good.

3 → He has forbidden his Governors to pass Laws of immediate and pressing importance, unless suspended in their operation till his Assent should be obtained; and when so suspended, he has utterly neglected to attend to them.

He has refused to pass other Laws for the accommodation of large districts of people, unless those people would relinquish the right of Representation in the Legislature, a right inestimable to them and formidable to tyrants only.

He has called together legislative bodies at places unusual, uncomfortable, and distant from

4 Defense: What the Colonists Did

This section has two paragraphs that rehearse the colonists' repeated efforts to peacefully address their concerns with the King.

4 → IN every stage of these Oppressions We have Petitioned for Redress in the most humble terms: Our repeated Petitions have been answered only by repeated injury. A Prince whose character is thus marked by every act which may define a Tyrant, is unfit to be the ruler of a free people.

Nor have We been wanting in attentions to our British brethren. We have warned them from time to time of attempts by their legislature to extend an

5 Declaration: We Stand Independent

This is the colonists' actual declaration of independence. It is their formal announcement that as of July 4, 1776 they considered themselves free from the ruling power of the British Crown and free from all political control by Great Britain. It took an eight-year war to prove it, but in the end, the colonists won.

5 → WE, therefore, the Representatives of the UNITED STATES OF AMERICA, in General Congress, Assembled, appealing to the Supreme Judge of the world for the rectitude of our intentions, do, in the Name, and by Authority of the good People of these Colonies, solemnly publish and declare, That these United Colonies are, and of Right ought to be Free and Independent States; that they are Absolved from all Allegiance to the British Crown, and that all political connection

THE CHARGES

The Declaration of Independence charged King George III and his government with using seven enemies of freedom to abuse and force the colonists to obey him. These *Seven Pillars of Tyranny* are ancient. They can be found in every harsh and despotic government since the dawn of history.

1. **All-powerful Ruler**: Freedom's greatest enemy is the all-powerful ruler. This can be an individual or a group. The ruler is beholden to no law, no governing body, and certainly not to the people themselves. His power is not limited. It is rule by supreme selfishness: "The king giveth and the king taketh away."
2. **Castes**: A ruler rewards his supporters by protecting them in a special elitist class with favors and privileges that others can't enjoy.
3. **Things in Common**: When rulers take over a nation's economy, they promise fairness by taking from the "have's" and giving to the "have not's."

The Framers called this "leveling," and warned future Americans against it. If such policies are allowed to run their course, they ultimately impoverish everyone.

4. **Regulation**: In an attempt to make possible "all things in common," rulers demand the power to regulate, set all prices, and tightly control all production and distribution.
5. **Force**: The people don't have a choice about the ruler's commands. His orders are imposed by force.
6. **Information**: The ruler controls the information flow so the people are led to believe the old way was bad and their new way is good—or will be soon.
7. **No Rights**: The ruler violates the people's rights whenever they stand in the way of his goals.

The Seven Pillars of Tyranny

The seven enemies of freedom can be seen in operation throughout history under an assortment of names and titles: communism, socialism, Nazism, totalitarianism, fascism, democratic socialism, dynasties, theocracies, Caesar, Pharaoh, Emperor, Czar, USSR, etc. Their names are different but in the end they each take power and control by wielding these same Seven Pillars of Tyranny.

TIMED READING

Read the Declaration From Start to Finish

This exercise takes less than 15 minutes.

Materials Needed:

A red pen, pencil or highlighter, and a timer
A copy of the Declaration of Independence (page 137)

Setting

Sit at a table or desk in a quiet well-lit place where you may easily underline and make notes.

Underlining

As you read, underline a few key words that bring to mind any of the Seven Pillars of Tyranny. Or, mark the words you don't understand and check the glossary.

Timed Exercise

This first time reading through the Declaration might be a little slow because the material is new. Start at the "When in the Course" and stop when you reach "...our sacred Honor."

Ready? Begin: Start the timer and begin reading.

Did you finish? Congratulations, you just read the Declaration of Independence.

Time: ________ Date: ________________

TEST YOURSELF

Helpful Details

Now that you have a general understanding of how the Declaration of Independence was written and organized, the answers to the following questions will not be difficult to find.

1. When did the Continental Congress sign the Declaration of Independence? ___________________

Preamble: "WHEN in the course ..."

2. From whom were the colonists dissolving their political bands? ______________________________

3. In the words of the Declaration, what does a people assume (receive) from the Powers of the Earth?

   ____

4. In the phrase "separate and equal Station," the word "separate" means individual, not combined. The words "equal Station" mean sharing the same circumstances

on earth. What do individuals share equally with all others on earth? HUMAN___________

5. Who is described as the author of these human rights? ________________________________

Assertion: "WE hold these Truths ..."

6. What does *self-evident* mean? ___________________

   ____

7. What does *unalienable* mean?__________________

8. For what purpose are "Governments instituted among Men"? _______________________________

9. Where should these governments rightfully get all their power and authority?

   ____

10. Do the people have the unalienable right to replace bad, broken or abusive governments? _______ Should that happen frequently? _______

11. The phrase "Mankind are more disposed to suffer ... than to right themselves" means that people are willing to put up with bad government so long as their basic needs are being satisfied. If government abuse won't stop what is the people's "right and duty"?

    ____

    ____

Charges: "HE has refused …."

12. With a pencil please number the first 13 Charges. They all begin with "He has." In that list,
    a. how many times is "refused" used? ___________
    b. how many times is "forbidden" used? _________
    c. how many times is "obstructed" used? _________

13. With a pencil resume numbering the Charges. After Charge #13 there are several that begin with "For."
    a. How many begin with "For"? _______
    b. In #17, "imposing Taxes" was done without what from the people? ____________________
    c. In #21, what "most valuable" thing did the King abolish? ___________________

14. In #23, the King is accused of refusing to defend the colonies and starting ________________________

15. In #27, the King is charged with inciting attacks from the frontiers from ___________________________

Defense: "IN every stage …"

16. There are two paragraphs in the Defense section. In the first, what did the colonists petition for?

    ____

17. Were their petitions answered? _______

18. In the last sentence, how did the colonists

estimate King George III as a Ruler of a free People?________________________________

19. In the second paragraph the colonists called upon their "Ties of our ________________________________" to stop the oppression. Did that succeed? _______

Declaration: "WE, therefore, ..."

20. After the second use of "Free and Independent States," the colonists claimed "full power" to:
    a. ____
    b. ____
    c. ____
    d. ____
    e. ____

21. Near the end of the Declaration the colonists stated a "firm Reliance on the Protection of divine Providence." To whom are they referring? __________
____

22. The British penalty for high treason was to be hanged by the head until unconscious. Then, cut down and revived. Then, disemboweled and beheaded. Then, cut into quarters, boiled in oil, and scattered abroad. To this possible ending the signers assembled pledged their
________________________, ____________________,
and their ______________________.

HISTORICAL BASICS
Of the Declaration of Independence

Purpose: To declare the separation of the colonies from Britain, to present their case for separation to the world, and to persuade fellow colonists and friendly foreign powers to unite in the cause.

Author, First draft: Thomas Jefferson, June 12-27, 1776

First Edit: John Adams, Benjamin Franklin, Roger Sherman, and Robert Livingston, June 27-28, 1776

Final Edit: Congress, July 1-4, 1776

Word count: 1,337 (1,480 with signatures)

Officially Adopted: July 4, 1776

Signed: Most of the delegates signed the Declaration on August 2, 1776. Five others signed at later dates, and two not at all.

Parchment: One sheet, 24-1/4 in. wide by 29-3/4 in. high

The document the delegates signed was engrossed on parchment. Engrossed means to make a copy in large, legible script to stand as the final version, the official copy. Parchment is a stiff, flat, thin, and durable material made from animal skin, usually sheep, calves or goats.

Signers: 56 members of Congress serving as delegates from the original thirteen colonies

October 20, 1774: The First Continental Congress creates the Continental Association to implement a trade boycott against the British. This united effort emboldened the colonists, and served as a direct precursor to the Declaration of Independence.

May 15, 1776: The Continental Congress advised the colonies that reconciliation with Britain was impossible and to start forming governments, write new constitutions, and change themselves from colonies to states.

July 2, 1776: Congress declares independence

July 4, 1776: Congress adopts the Declaration of Independence

July 4, 1776: John Dunlap prints about 200 copies, now known as the "Dunlap Broadsides"; 24 are known to exist.

July 6, 1776: Pennsylvania Evening Post of July 6 prints the first newspaper rendition

July 8, 1776: The first public reading is in Philadelphia.

July 9, 1776: Washington orders it to be read before the American army in New York

July 19, 1776: Congress orders the Declaration of Independence engrossed and signed by members.

August 2, 1776: Delegates begin to sign the engrossed copy of the Declaration. At the same time a large British reinforcement arrives at New York after it was repelled at Charleston, S.C.

January 18, 1777: Congress's new headquarters is now in Baltimore, Maryland. They send orders that signed copies of the Declaration, printed by Mary Katherine Goddard of Baltimore, be sent to all the colonies.

Making King George III Unconstitutional

When the Americans won their independence they wanted to make sure the King's abusive behavior would not be repeated in the United States. The Framers wanted their new Constitution to create limits, checks and balances so the President could never act like a tyrannical king.

Listed below are the 27 charges made against the King, and more than 50 places in the Constitution where those abuses are made illegal. Each charge is presented in three parts:

Part 1: A summary headline of the King's deplorable act.

Part 2: The actual complaint or charge, as written by Thomas Jefferson in the Declaration.

Part 3: The Constitution's solution, with citations.

The colonists used the word "King" to include King George III himself, as well as his ministers, members of Parliament, and royally-appointed local leaders, all of whom tried to force the Americans to submit to British rule.

1. The King prevented passage of laws which the people wanted and needed.

Declaration: *"He has refused his Assent to Laws, the most wholesome and necessary for the public good."*

Constitution: The President must enforce the laws passed by Congress. If he believes a law is harmful to the United States he may veto (reject) it, but Congress can force it into law by a two-thirds majority vote.
(See Article III, Section 3; Article I, Section 7, Clause 2)

2. The King suspended new laws until he personally approved them.

Declaration: *"He has forbidden his Governors to pass Laws of immediate and pressing importance, unless suspended in their operation till his Assent should be obtained; and when so suspended, he has utterly neglected to attend to them."*

Constitution: The President has only ten days to review a bill. If he does not respond within ten days, it automatically becomes law. If he vetoes it, a two-thirds majority vote by Congress can override his veto.
(See Article I, Section 7, Clause 2)

3. The King would not allow new representatives into the assemblies.

Declaration: *"He has refused to pass other Laws for the accommodation of large districts of people, unless those people would relinquish the right of Representation in the Legislature, a right inestimable to them and formidable to tyrants only."*

Constitution: The President has no power to prevent new states from forming, or to prevent the people from

electing local and federal representatives.
(See Article IV, Section 3, Clause 1; Article IV, Section 4)

4. The King forced the assemblies to meet in difficult locations.

Declaration: *"He has called together legislative bodies at places unusual, uncomfortable, and distant from the depository of their Public Records, for the sole purpose of fatiguing them into compliance with his measures."*

Constitution: The President has no power to tell Congress or the state legislatures where to meet. Congress must meet in Washington, D.C.
(See Article I, Section 5 and Section 8, Clause 17; Amendment X)

5. The King dismissed the people's assemblies repeatedly.

Declaration: *"He has dissolved Representative Houses repeatedly, for opposing with manly firmness of his invasions on the rights of the people."*

Constitution: The President has no power to dissolve Congress or to arrest its members. Only Congress has power to decide when to adjourn.
(See Article I, Section 2, Clause 3; Article I, Section 4, Clause 2; Article I, Section 5; Article I, Section 6, Clause 1)

6. The King prevented the people from electing new assemblies.

Declaration: *"He has refused for a long time, after such dissolutions, to cause others to be elected, whereby the Legislative*

Powers, incapable of Annihilation, have returned to the People at large for their exercise; the State remaining in the mean time exposed to all the dangers of invasion from without, and convulsions within."

Constitution: The President has no power to prevent the states from electing local and federal representatives.

(See Article I, Section 3, Clause 1; Article I, Section 4, Clause 1)

7. The King thwarted immigration and homesteading.

Declaration: *"He has endeavoured to prevent the population of these States; for that purpose obstructing the Laws for Naturalization of Foreigners; refusing to pass others to encourage their migrations hither, and raising the conditions of new Appropriations of Lands."*

Constitution: The President has no power to interfere with routine immigration, or to interfere with the parceling out of land for new settlers.

(See Article I, Section 8, Clause 4; Article IV, Section 3, Clause 2)

8. The King refused to let the colonies create courts of justice.

Declaration: *"He has obstructed the Administration of Justice by refusing his Assent to Laws for establishing Judiciary Powers."*

Constitution: The President cannot interfere with Congress establishing courts on the federal level, or states on their level. The Tenth Amendment empowers the states to create their own court system.

(See Article III, Section 1and 2; Article I, Section 8, Clause 9; Amendment X)

9. The King coerced judges to obey his will or be fired.

Declaration: *"He has made Judges dependent on his Will alone for the tenure of their offices, and the amount and payment of their salaries."*

Constitution: The President may nominate judges but he can't tamper with their employment. Only Congress is empowered to set salaries and remove a judge using the impeachment process.

(See Article III, Section 1; Article I, Section 2, Clause 5; Article I, Section 3, Clause 6)

10. The King added bureaucrats without benefit to the public.

Declaration: *"He has erected a multitude of New Offices, and sent hither swarms of Officers to harass our people and eat out their substance."*

Constitution: This charge was in regard to new bureaucrats sent to enforce trade law. Only Congress may regulate international trade. The President may not add bureaucrats without congressional approval. Congress has power to choose which of his nominations should require congressional approval.

(See Article 1, Section 8, Clause 3; Article II, Section 2)

11. The King forced standing armies without consent.

Declaration: *"He has kept among us, in times of peace, Standing Armies without the Consent of our legislatures."*

Constitution: The President has no power to station troops among the people without congressional approval. Only Congress has power to establish, fund,

make rules and regulate the armed forces.
(See Amendment III; Article 1, Section 8, Clauses 12-16)

12. He made the military superior to civil authority.

Declaration: *"He has affected to render the Military independent of and superior to the Civil Power."*

Constitution: The military is kept under civilian control with the President (a civilian) as its Commander in Chief. Only Congress may establish, fund, make rules and regulate the armed forces.
(See Article II, Section 2, Clause 1; Article VI, Clause 2; Section 8, Clauses 12-16)

13. The King allowed Parliament to impose its will without consent.

Declaration: *"He has combined with others to subject us to a jurisdiction foreign to our constitution, and unacknowledged by our laws; giving his Assent to their Acts of pretended Legislation."*

Constitution: The President has no power to take judicial or legislative action in violation of the separation of powers as spelled out in the Constitution.
(See Article I, Section 1; Article III, Section 1)

14. The King forced colonists to house armed soldiers.

Declaration: *"For quartering large bodies of armed troops among us."*

Constitution: The President has no power to force citizens to house soldiers in their homes.
(See Amendment III)

15. The King protected his soldiers from punishment for murders.

Declaration: *"For protecting them, by a mock Trial from punishment for any Murders which they should commit on the Inhabitants of these States."*

Constitution: The President may not interfere with accused criminals being tried in a public trial in the state where the crime occurred, or where Congress may decide. He may grant reprieves and pardons afterward, but pardons should be rare and given only for justifiable reasons.

(See Article III, Section 2, Clause 3; Article II, Section 2, Clause 1)

16. The King cut off trade with all parts of the world.

Declaration: *"For cutting off our Trade with all parts of the world."*

Constitution: The President has no power to regulate international and national trade, a power reserved for Congress alone.

(See Article I, Section 8, Clause 3)

17. The King created new taxes without the colonists' consent.

Declaration: *"For imposing Taxes on us without our Consent."*

Constitution: The President has no power to tax the people. Only Congress has power to tax.

(See Article I, Section 8, Clause 1)

18. The King deprived the colonists of trial by jury.

Declaration: *"For depriving us in many cases, of the benefit of Trial by Jury."*

Constitution: Defendants in criminal cases must be tried by an impartial jury.

(See Article III, Section 2, Clause 3; Amendment VI)

19. The King forced accused Americans to be tried in British courts.

Declaration: *"For transporting us beyond Seas to be tried for pretended offences."*

Constitution: Defendants are guaranteed the right to a speedy and public trial by an impartial jury of the state and district where the crime occurred, and to have the assistance of counsel for his defense.

(See Amendment VI; Article III, Section 2, Clause 3)

20. The King expanded Quebec's borders into northern colonies.

Declaration: *"For abolishing the free System of English Laws in a neighbouring Province, establishing therein an Arbitrary government, and enlarging its Boundaries so as to render it at once an example and fit instrument for introducing the same absolute rule into these Colonies."*

Constitution: The President has no power to take territory from states or to control other property belonging to the United States. This power is granted solely to Congress.

(See Article IV, Section 3, Clause 2)

21. The King rescinded century-old royal charters, destroyed local law.

Declaration*: "For taking away our Charters, abolishing our most valuable Laws and altering fundamentally the Forms of our Governments."*

Constitution: The President has no power to destroy the supreme law of the land, namely the Constitution, or state laws.

(See Article VI, Clause 2; Article IV)

22. The King assumed all legislative power without consent.

Declaration*: "For suspending our own Legislatures, and declaring themselves invested with power to legislate for us in all cases whatsoever."*

Constitution: The President has no power to make law, violate separation of powers, destroy state sovereignty, or violate local state law.

(See Article I, II, III, IV)

23. The King refused to defend the colonies from attack.

Declaration*: "He has abdicated Government here, by declaring us out of his Protection and waging War against us."*

Constitution: The U.S. government guarantees to every state in the union protection from invasion and domestic violence.

(See Article IV, Section 4)

24. The King committed open assault against the Americans.

Declaration: *"He has plundered our seas, ravaged our coasts, burnt our towns, and destroyed the lives of our people."*

Constitution: The President may not levy war against the states, help their enemies, or give aid and comfort to enemies of the United States, nor may he deprive any citizen of life, liberty or property without due process of law.

(See Article III, Section 3, Clause 1; Amendment V)

25. The King hired foreign troops to beat the colonists into submission.

Declaration: *"He is at this time transporting large Armies of foreign Mercenaries to compleat the works of death, desolation, and tyranny, already begun with circumstances of Cruelty & Perfidy scarcely paralleled in the most barbarous ages, and totally unworthy the Head of a civilized nation."*

Constitution: The President may not militarily occupy U.S. territory or arbitrarily direct military action against citizens without approval of Congress and with due process of law.

(See Amendment III and V)

26. The King kidnapped Americans at sea and forced them to join British.

Declaration: *"He has constrained our fellow Citizens taken Captive on the high Seas to bear Arms against their Country, to become the executioners of their friends and Brethren, or to fall themselves by their Hands."*

Constitution: The President is not granted direct police power to arrest, and must always follow due process of law. Congress has sole power to make rules concerning captures on land and water.

(See Article I, Section 8, Clause 11; Amendment X and V)

27. The King incited class warfare, internal strife, war with American Indians.

Declaration: *"He has excited domestic insurrections amongst us, and has endeavoured to bring on the inhabitants of our frontiers, the merciless Indian Savages whose known rule of warfare, is an undistinguished destruction of all ages, sexes and conditions."*

Constitution: Congress has sole power to declare war. By law the President may not stir up turmoil or initiate war.

(See Article IV, Section 4; Article I, Section 8, Clause 11)

PART III

THE CONSTITUTION

WHAT DO I NEED TO KNOW?

Reading the Constitution does not take a great deal of preparation.

You don't need to know a lot of history or economics or political science to read the Constitution for the first time. However, the reasons for many of its provisions will not become clear until the context of its creation is understood. That's why the Declaration of Independence is so helpful. Knowing the kinds of misery and torment that monarchs can create while governing others can help explain why certain government duties are spelled out in detail in the Constitution, and others are not.

For now, be aware that there have been two versions of the Constitution adopted in the U.S.

1st Version Didn't Work—1777–1787

The Framers created their first constitution during the War for Independence. They called it the Articles of Confederation, and wrote it in 1777. It was ratified (adopted) in 1781, shortly before the war ended.

The Articles failed because they didn't give the central government enough power to force the states to work together to end the war quickly. The Articles created confusion and frustration instead of one unified and strong nation.

2nd Version Almost Perfect—1787

In the summer of 1787, delegates from the 13 states met in Philadelphia to repair the Articles. When it was clear the Articles simply wouldn't work, the Framers replaced them with a far more effective document.

It took them four months to fashion a new form of government that was friendly to the people. It created three branches of government with checks and balances on each other's powers. It put control into the hands of the people through representatives. It established a court to solve legal challenges. It shared the power between the people, the states, and the federal government in a fair and balanced manner. That's the version that thrust the United States into its period of greatest freedom, growth and expansion.

Can't Be Ignorant and Free

One of the Framers, Thomas Jefferson, said, "If a nation expects to be ignorant and free, in a state of civilization, it expects what never was and never will be."

In other words, the Framers warned that being ignorant of how freedom works will eventually lead to the loss of that freedom.

James Madison said it another way: "I believe there are more instances of the abridgment of freedom of the people by gradual and silent encroachments by those in power than by violent and sudden usurpations."

Thomas Jefferson encouraged all Americans to be good custodians of their hard-earned freedom: "The price of liberty is eternal vigilance," he said. The word "vigilance" means to keep careful watch for possible danger or difficulties.

A Good First Step

There are thousands of books that beautifully explain the history and creation of the Constitution. They quote the original thinkers and tell about the many varied sources from which the Framers found guidance and understanding. They tell about the wars for freedom, and the great debates to find that perfect balance between all power in a ruler and no government power at all. They tell the exciting story of how the Framers created the world's first free society.

Learning that story is critically important. However, most people just want to know where to begin. Where can Americans turn to learn how freedom and liberty really work, and understand the valuable role filled by the Constitution?

The answer is in the Constitution itself—by asking the right questions and by applying the answers to current events. Begin by taking this short tour through the Constitution.

STRUCTURE

How is the Constitution Organized?

The Constitution is neatly organized like a book with Chapters, Paragraphs, and Sentences. In the Constitution these three levels are called Articles, Sections, and Clauses.

1 **Articles.**

The main chapters are called Articles. There are seven Articles that are numbered using Roman numerals (I, II, III, etc.).

2 **Sections.**

Each Article is divided into small Sections. A Section has one or more paragraphs. These are numbered with Arabic numerals (1, 2, 3, etc.).

3 **Clauses.**

Clauses are single sentences or a paragraph. They are not numbered but people refer to them in the order they appear: The first paragraph is called Clause 1, the second is Clause 2, etc.

NICKNAMES

Many of the Clauses are talked about so frequently that they are now best known by their nicknames. For example, the Commerce Clause, the War Clause, the Supremacy Clause, the Establishment Clause, the Due Process Clause etc.

Preamble

1

2

3

CONSTITUTION OF THE UNITED STATES

WE THE PEOPLE of the United States, in Order to form a more perfect Union, establish Justice, insure domestic Tranquility, provide for the common defense, promote the general Welfare, and secure the Blessings of Liberty to ourselves and our Posterity, do ordain and establish this Constitution for the United States of America.

Article. I.

SECTION. 1. All legislative Powers herein granted shall be vested in a Congress of the United States, which shall consist of a Senate and House of Representatives.

SECTION. 2. The House of Representatives shall be composed of Members chosen every second Year by the People of the several States, and the Electors in each State shall have the Qualifications requisite for Electors of the most numerous Branch of the State Legislature.

No Person shall be a Representative who shall not have attained to the Age of twenty five Years, and been seven Years a Citizen of the United States, and who shall not, when elected, be an Inhabitant of that State in which he shall be chosen.

[Representatives and direct Taxes shall be apportioned among the several States which may be included within this Union, according to their respective Numbers, which shall be determined by adding to the whole Number of free Persons, including those bound to Service for a Term of Years, and excluding Indians not taxed, three fifths of all other Persons.]* The actual Enumeration shall be made within

*Changed by section 2 of the Fourteenth Amendment

CONTENT

How is the Information Arranged?

The first three Articles set up the three great branches of government. These are carefully interwoven as separate but unified groups. Powerful checks and balances are included so the branches can't abuse their powers. The last four Articles deal with the states and the methods and processes needed to make it all work.

1 **Article 1. Legislature**

All power to make laws is given to the Legislative Branch, also called Congress. The Congress is divided into two parts—the House of Representatives and the Senate. Their job is to create all the laws, and to control the money.

2 **Article 2. Executive**

The Executive Branch is the President and all of the agencies and departments in the government. It is responsible for enforcing the laws passed by Congress.

3 **Article 3. Judiciary**

The Judicial Branch is the Supreme Court

and all the lower federal courts. Their job is to decide if the laws and actions of citizens and the government are in harmony with the Constitution. The Constitution set up the Supreme Court and gave Congress the responsibility to set up lower courts as needed.

Article I

1 → **SECTION 1.** All legislative Powers herein granted shall be vested in a Congress of the United States, which shall consist of a Senate and House of Representatives.

SECTION 2. The House of Representatives shall

Article II

2 → **SECTION 1.** The executive Power shall be vested in a President of the United States of America. He shall hold his Office during the Term of four Years, and, together with the Vice President, chosen for the same Term, be elected, as follows

Each State shall appoint, in such Manner as the

Article III

3 → **SECTION 1.** The judicial Power of the United States, shall be vested in one supreme Court, and in such inferior Courts as the Congress may from time to time ordain and establish. The Judges, both of the supreme and inferior Courts, shall hold their Offices during good Behavior, and shall, at stated

4 Article 4. States

The states are individually controlled by their own governments. The Constitution gives the states certain powers and responsibilities toward each other and toward the federal government. Working separately or working together, the states form a formidable power for prosperity, trade, and national security.

5 Article 5. Amendments

This Article provides a peaceful means to improve and perpetuate the Constitution. The process of amending is made cumbersome because proposed changes should be heavily scrutinized, and never adopted recklessly. The Framers wanted the eternal principles of freedom to remain intact and immune from being accidentally or intentionally amended away.

6 Article 6. Supremacy

This Article makes it clear there must be one supreme standard of law, and that is the Constitution. Every elected person is beholden to the Constitution by oath or affirmation. The Framers wrote frequently about the need for honesty in all levels of government, and among the people themselves, as a necessary ingredient for self-government and lasting freedom.

Article IV

4 **SECTION 1** Full Faith and Credit shall be given in each State to the public Acts, Records, and judicial Proceedings of every other State. And the Congress may by general Laws prescribe the

Article V

The Congress, whenever two thirds of both Houses shall deem it necessary, shall propose Amendments 5 to this Constitution, or, on the Application of the Legislatures of two thirds of the several States, shall call a Convention for proposing Amendments, which, in either Case, shall be valid to all Intents

Article VI

All Debts contracted and Engagements entered into, before the Adoption of this Constitution, shall be as valid against the United States under this Constitution, as under the Confederation.

6 This Constitution and the Laws of the United States which shall be made in Pursuance thereof; and all Treaties made, or which shall be made, under the Authority of the United States, shall be the supreme Law of the Land; and the Judges in every State shall be bound thereby, any Thing in

7 Article 7. Ratification

This Article declares that nine of the states would be sufficient to ratify the new Constitution.

Article VII

7 The Ratification of the Conventions of nine States, shall be sufficient for the Establishment of this Constitution between the States so ratifying

AMENDMENTS

How are Changes Displayed?

Over the years the seven Articles of the Constitution have had some wording changes. Most copies of the Constitution show those changes by wrapping the original wording inside brackets. Sometimes they include a little footnote to point out that change.

CONSTITUTION OF THE UNITED STATES

WE THE PEOPLE of the United States, in Order to form a more perfect Union, establish Justice, insure domestic Tranquility, provide for the common defense, promote the general Welfare, and secure the Blessings of Liberty to ourselves and our Posterity, do ordain and establish this Constitution for the United States of America.

Article. I.

SECTION. 1. All legislative Powers herein granted shall be vested in a Congress of the United States, which shall consist of a Senate and House of Representatives.

SECTION. 2. The House of Representatives shall be composed of Members chosen every second Year by the People of the several States, and the Electors in each State shall have the Qualifications requisite for Electors of the most numerous Branch of the State Legislature.

No Person shall be a Representative who shall not have attained to the Age of twenty five Years, and been seven Years a Citizen of the United States, and who shall not, when elected, be an Inhabitant of that State in which he shall be chosen.

[Representatives and direct Taxes shall be apportioned among the several States which may be included within this Union, according to their respective Numbers, which shall be determined by adding to the whole Number of free Persons, including those bound to Service for a Term of Years, and excluding Indians not taxed, three fifths of all other Persons.]* The actual Enumeration shall be made within

*Changed by section 2 of the Fourteenth Amendment

FOOTNOTES

How do Publications Show Citations?

There's one symbol that many people may not recognize when it comes to citing the Constitution in footnotes. It's the symbol for Section: §

Formal publications use §, but most just spell it out.

To equate justice under the law.

71 N. McFetridge, Calvinism in History 74 (Quoted

72 Diamond, The Declaration and the Constitution: Liberty, Pub. Interest 46-48 (Fall 1975)

73 U. S. Const. art. I, §9

See also

Article I, Section 3, Clause 3 (Three-fifths Clause)
Article I, Section 8, Clause 3 (Commerce with Foreign Nations)
Article I, Section 8, Clause 3 (Commerce Among the States)
Article IV, Section 2, Clause 3 (Fugitive Slave Clause)

MEMORY TRICK

How to Remember the Seven Articles

Is there a convenient way to remember what each of the seven Articles describes?

In this era of modern pop-culture movies, a whole generation of alien-sounding outer space names have entered the vernacular.

In all of these wonderful and creative names who has ever heard of Lej Sasr?

Probably no one because he is a made-up character to help people remember the seven Articles. Say his name twice a day for a week and it won't be forgotten—L.E.J. S.A.S.R.

L — Legislative Branch, Article I

E — Executive Branch, Article II

J — Judicial Branch, Article III

S — States, Article IV

A — Amendments, Article V

S — Supreme Law, Article VI

R — Ratification, Article VII

LEJ SASR

TIMED READING

Read the Seven Articles From Start to Finish

This exercise takes 30-45 minutes.

Materials Needed:

A red pen, pencil or highlighter, and a timer
A copy of the Constitution (see page 145)

Setting

Sit at a table or desk in a quiet well-lit place where you may easily underline and make notes.

Underlining

As you read, underline 2-3 key words that bring to mind the meaning of a sentence or paragraph. Or, mark any words you don't understand and check the glossary.

Timed Exercise

Reading through the Constitution for the first time might be a little slow because the material is new. Start at the Preamble and stop when you reach the end of Article VII and the name of George Washington.

Ready? Begin: Start the timer and begin reading.

Did you finish? Congratulations, you just read the U.S. Constitution.

Time: ________ Date: ________________

TEST YOURSELF

Helpful Details

Now that you have a general understanding of how the Constitution is formed and organized, the answers to the following questions will not be difficult to find.

1. How many Articles are there? ______

2. Which is the longest Article? ______

3. Which is the shortest Article? ______

4. Which Article has the most Sections? ______

5. Which Articles have no numbered Sections? ______

6. In some books and articles, this unusual symbol, §, is used to direct readers to a certain part of the Constitution. What is that part?

   ____

7. What three divisions in the Constitution are used as the "address" to locate information?

   ______________ ______________ ______________

8. What space-alien name helps recall the main purpose of each Article? ______________________________

9. How is the original wording set apart when Amendments have changed the text? (For an example see Article I, Section 2, clause 3.) __________________

10. Which Branch makes the laws? _________________

11. Which Branch enforces the laws? ________________

12. Which Branch decides if laws are constitutional?

    ____

13. Which Article describes how the President is elected to office? ________

14. Which Article describes how a new state may enter the union? ________

15. Which Article describes how to change the Constitution? ________

16. Which Article explains what must happen to make the Constitution the law of the land? ________

17. Opinion question: Why do you suppose the Framers wanted the state legislatures to appoint the Senators instead of having them elected by popular vote? (See Article I, Section 3, Clause 1)

18. Please read the Thomas Jefferson quote on page v to answer the following:
    a. Who are the real guardians of the Constitution?

       ____

    b. Did Jefferson say the government was the best "depository of the ultimate powers of the society"?

       ____

    c. Should some freedoms be removed from the people if they don't control them with care and "discretion"?

       ____

    d. What single word describes the best remedy to correct abuses of constitutional power? __________

The Bill of Rights

The following section introduces the Bill of Rights. This is the first ten amendments, the part of the Constitution that most people know of, identify with, and remember the best.

PART IV

THE BILL OF RIGHTS & AMENDMENTS 11–27

THE BILL OF RIGHTS

Protecting Human Rights

Article I Section 8 of the Constitution gives the federal government only 20 powers. It has no authority to violate a person's human rights such as freedom of religion, press, assembly, petition, etc. Neither is there any federal authority granted to abolish free speech, invade privacy, impose cruel punishment, etc.

Bill of Rights Not Necessary?

The problem for some of the Framers in 1787 was a distrust of the federal government to respect unwritten rights. They feared that if human rights were not written down, conspiring men would pick and choose at their convenience what they considered valid human rights.

Danger of Making a List

The Constitution is a declaration of almost 300 rights. Some of the Framers believed that adding to this a separate list of rights might leave some rights forgotten and left out—a lapse that might be used by the government to abuse the people at some future time. In spite of this, the people wanted a written Bill of Rights.

Hundreds of Ideas

After the Constitution was ratified, a total of 189 suggested amendments were submitted to Congress to create a Bill of Rights. James Madison boiled them down to 17, but Congress approved only 12 of them. The states ratified 10, making the Bill of Rights the law of the land on December 15, 1791.

Not a Declaration of New Rights

The Bill of Rights is not a list of new rights or a declaration of every claimed right. Every human right has *always* existed because every living soul is "endowed by their Creator with certain unalienable rights," as the Declaration of Independence stated.

Instead, the Bill of Rights lists what the federal government may *not* do. It is a list of restraints to prevent the government from abusing human rights.

What Is a Right?

A "right" is a legal or ethical entitlement. The Framers identified two basic rights: (1) those legal rights granted by the government, and (2) those natural or unalienable rights that are gifts from the Creator. Many people confuse the two, thinking that some parts of life should automatically be theirs by simply making the claim. What are the differences between legal and natural rights?

Legal Rights

Legal rights are granted by the government. They are the customs and rules that allow people to interact together without injuring each other in the process.

For example, legal rights include the right to operate a car, vote, build a house, patent an idea, drive on a road, dispense medicine to a paying public, broadcast a radio or television signal, cross borders, participate in health insurance, copyright music, sell paintings, start a business, and go fishing.

Legal rights have three qualities:

1. **Selective**: Legal rights are selective. Not everyone may have or receive the identical rights.
2. **Temporary**: The government grants them according to laws and rules on which everyone agrees.
3. **Responsibility**: If certain rules and regulations are not met, the people empower the government to revoke the legal rights and punish the violator in order to keep the peace.

Natural Rights

On the other hand, natural or unalienable rights don't impose on others, and they are universal. Every person is born with them. They may not be revoked or legislated away.

An unalienable right has three qualities.

1. **Universal**: Every living soul is "endowed by their creator" with the same natural rights.

2. **Doesn't Impose**: Exercising a natural right imposes no obligation on another person. It does not infringe on the rights of other people.
3. **Responsibility**: A natural right carries the duty to use it respectfully. Rights must not be misused to cause harm.

There are at least 286 natural rights that are protected by the Constitution. There are probably other unalienable rights that have not been recognized because of world or cultural circumstances. They too will come to light one day because the struggle for freedom is the struggle to exercise unalienable rights.

CONTENT

The first ten Amendments are called the Bill of Rights. They list specific restrictions on the government so there is no ambiguity should abusive leaders try to create their own list of human rights.

First Amendment.

The First Amendment lists five basic rights which the government may not harm or diminish.

1 Religion

The Framers worried that Congress would force a national religion on the people, or prevent them from freely practicing their religion of choice. This Amendment forced Congress to mind its own business.

2 Speech and Press

Freedom of speech and press is not an exclusive right—there must remain reasonable restrictions (e.g., libel, slander, inciting riots). The Framers wanted the states to set those regulations.

3 Assembly

A major complaint against King George III was that his guards stopped or arrested people who gathered in groups, large or small, to talk. The Framers disallowed such harassment.

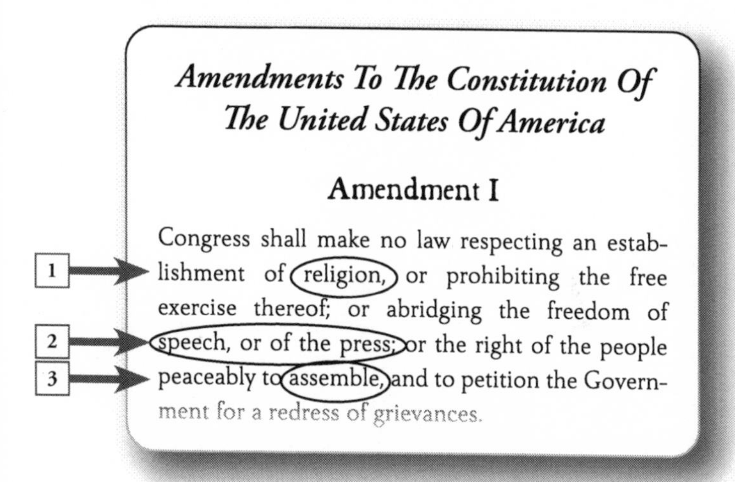
Amendments To The Constitution Of The United States Of America

Amendment I

Congress shall make no law respecting an establishment of religion, or prohibiting the free exercise thereof; or abridging the freedom of speech, or of the press; or the right of the people peaceably to assemble, and to petition the Government for a redress of grievances.

4 Petition the Government

The people have the right to challenge and confront the government without interference by the authorities.

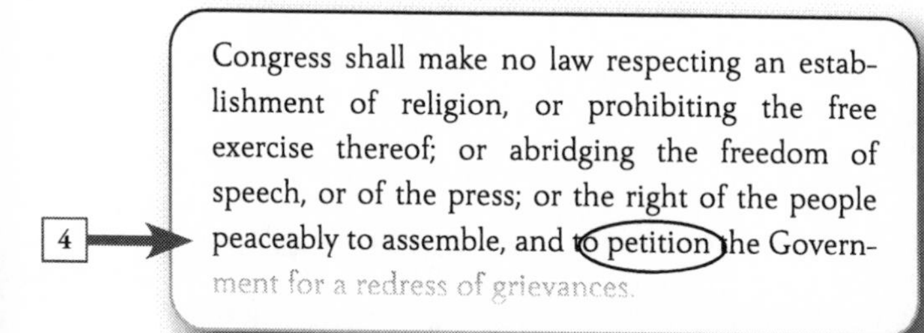
Congress shall make no law respecting an establishment of religion, or prohibiting the free exercise thereof; or abridging the freedom of speech, or of the press; or the right of the people peaceably to assemble, and to petition the Government for a redress of grievances.

Second Amendment.

The second amendment makes it clear that the federal government may not interfere with the citizens' right to own firearms.

5 Militia

The State Militia is a body of citizens which can be called up by the governor or Congress to protect the people from harm.

Many Americans confuse their State Militia with the National Guard, which is a separate reserve corps in each state trained at federal expense.

6 Right to keep and bear arms

The right to self-defense is a natural, unalienable right. Owning a firearm for self-defense was a longstanding right among the colonies before the Constitution was written. This amendment ensures the right to own firearms for personal protection, self-defense, and in service of the militia.

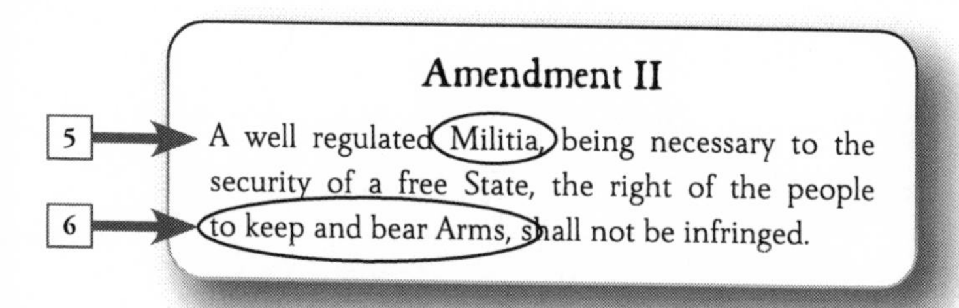

Amendment II

A well regulated Militia, being necessary to the security of a free State, the right of the people to keep and bear Arms, shall not be infringed.

Third Amendment.

7 No quartering of soldiers

This prevents the government from forcing citizens to house soldiers at their own expense in times of peace. In the 1770s, Americans had to provide food and bedding to the King's troops, and suffer the abuses that often followed—theft and destruction of property, ravishing of women, abusing the owners.

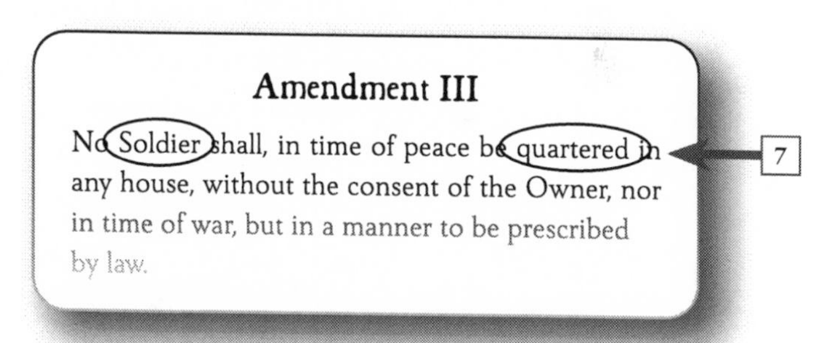

Amendment III

No Soldier shall, in time of peace be quartered in any house, without the consent of the Owner, nor in time of war, but in a manner to be prescribed by law.

Fourth Amendment.

This Amendment was written to keep the government from prying into people's personal lives, dwellings, and effects.

8 Privacy

The right to the privacy of homes, businesses and private papers ("to be secure") is protected in the Constitution to prevent the government from fishing for personal or illegal behavior without just cause or without due process of law.

9 Unreasonable Searches and Seizures

This provision protects people from unreasonable invasion of privacy and confiscation of private property. The police, for example, may gather evidence at a crime scene, or cross private property when pursuing a suspected criminal or to rescue a human life. However, they may not arbitrarily go searching around for violations of the law without just cause.

10 Warrant from Courts

A government officer may not arrest a citizen unless a warrant is issued by a judge. The exception is when a person is seen committing a crime and is apprehended by those who witnessed it.

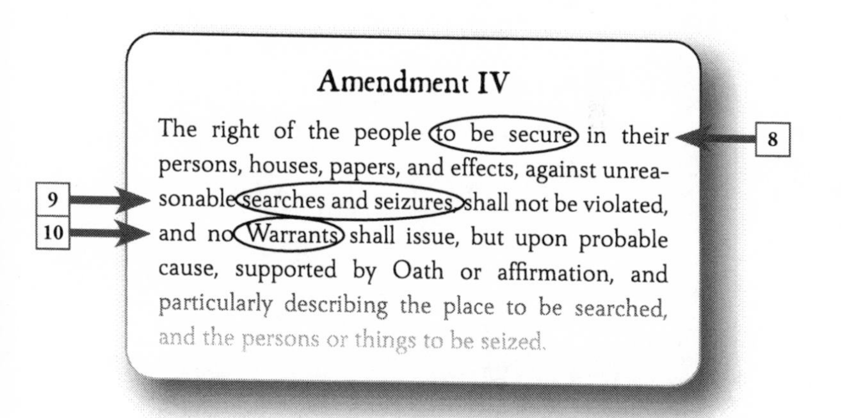

Fifth Amendment.

Many people have heard the phrase "I plead the fifth." That statement refers to the Fifth Amendment. A citizen cannot be forced to tell the court things that could get him thrown into jail.

11 Grand Jury

Before a person can be formally charged for a serious crime a grand jury must first hear the evidence and agree that an actual crime most likely did take place.

12 Can't Be Tried Twice

Once a person has been found innocent or guilty, he can't be tried for the same crime a second time.

13 Forced Confession

A person can't be forced to confess to a crime. He may volunteer the information in a plea deal, or confess it just to clear his conscience, but he can't be forced.

14 Due Process

This powerful protection prevents the government from taking an American's life, liberty or property without a hearing, known as "due process of law."

Amendment V

No person shall be held to answer for a capital, or otherwise infamous crime, unless on a presentment or indictment of a Grand Jury, except in cases arising in the land or naval forces, or in the Militia, when in actual service in time of War or public danger; nor shall any person be subject for the same offence to be twice put in jeopardy of life or limb; nor shall be compelled in any criminal case to be a witness against himself, nor be deprived of life, liberty, or property, without due process of law; nor shall private property be taken for public use, without just compensation.

11 — Grand Jury
12 — twice put
13 — witness against himself

15 Property Rights

The government may not take personal property without giving the owner fair payment or compensation. This kind of government "taking" is called exercising "eminent domain." It may not take place except to benefit the general public, and with fair compensation.

Amendment V

No person shall be held to answer for a capital, or otherwise infamous crime, unless on a presentment or indictment of a Grand Jury, except in cases arising in the land or naval forces, or in the Militia, when in actual service in time of War or public danger; nor shall any person be subject for the same offence to be twice put in jeopardy of life or limb; nor shall be compelled in any criminal case to be a witness against himself, nor be deprived of life, liberty, or property, without due process of law; nor shall private property be taken for public use, without just compensation.

14 — due process
15 — private property

Sixth Amendment.

The Framers were very leery of King George III's judicial system because he used it to silence or destroy his opposition. They went to great lengths to make sure this would not happen again.

16 Speedy Trial

A speedy and public trial also had to allow both sides enough time to prepare their cases properly. The trials are made public so others can make sure the trial is fair.

17 Impartial Jury

The accused has the right to be tried by his peers, who are selected from the area where the crime was committed. This is meant to protect the accused from bias and mobs.

18 Informed

Under British rule, prisoners were often denied learning what their formal charges were, and therefore couldn't prepare a proper defense. The Bill of Rights requires that a charge be clearly stated right away.

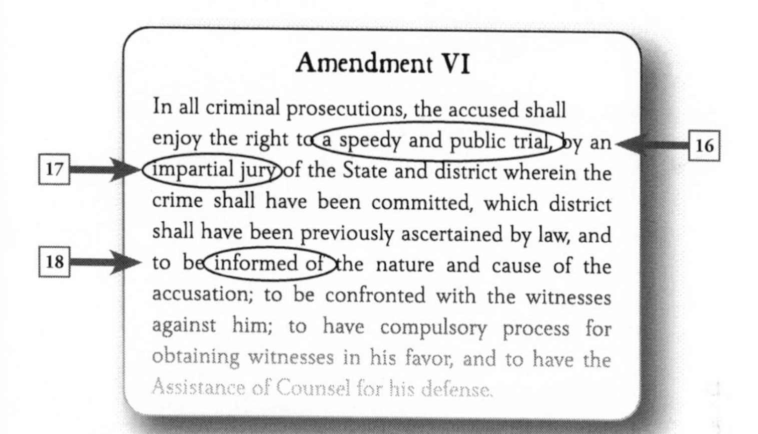
Amendment VI

In all criminal prosecutions, the accused shall enjoy the right to a speedy and public trial, by an impartial jury of the State and district wherein the crime shall have been committed, which district shall have been previously ascertained by law, and to be informed of the nature and cause of the accusation; to be confronted with the witnesses against him; to have compulsory process for obtaining witnesses in his favor, and to have the Assistance of Counsel for his defense.

19 Confront Witnesses

The accused may cross-examine a witness to discover if the witness's account is true or not. If no witness in his favor will come forward, the accused may use the subpoena system to compel witnesses to appear.

20 Right to Counsel

The accused is guaranteed a lawyer to represent him whether he can afford one or not.

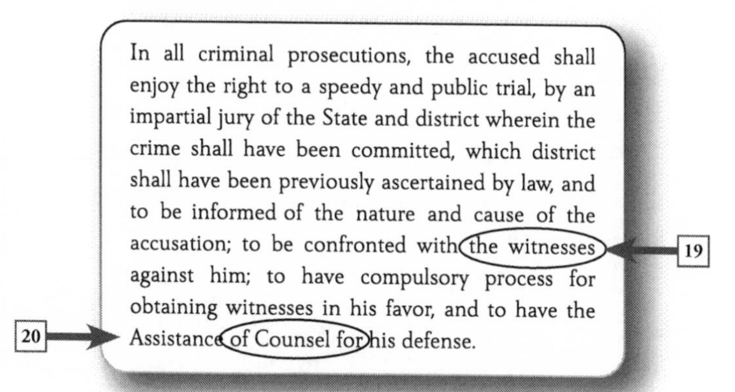
In all criminal prosecutions, the accused shall enjoy the right to a speedy and public trial, by an impartial jury of the State and district wherein the crime shall have been committed, which district shall have been previously ascertained by law, and to be informed of the nature and cause of the accusation; to be confronted with the witnesses against him; to have compulsory process for obtaining witnesses in his favor, and to have the Assistance of Counsel for his defense.

Seventh Amendment.

21 Trial by Jury

The Framers wanted to ensure that people seeking damages of $20 or more had the right to trial by jury.

22 Protecting Evidence

The decisions about facts and evidence made by one jury may not be undone by another. If a case is appealed, the new jury must accept the prior findings as fact.

Amendment VII

In Suits at common law, where the value in controversy shall exceed twenty dollars, the right of trial by jury shall be preserved, and no fact tried by a jury, shall be otherwise re-examined in any Court of the United States, than according to the rules of the common law.

21 → "of trial by jury"

22 → "re-examined"

Eighth Amendment.

23 Excessive Fines and Punishment

King George III abused the people with outlandish fines and enormous bails, preventing the people from working to pay them off. The Framers put a stop to that.

King George III also tortured criminals by cutting off ears, flogging, cutting off hands, castrating, standing them at the pillory for days, slitting the nose, branding, and letting them rot in prison. The Framers stopped that, too.

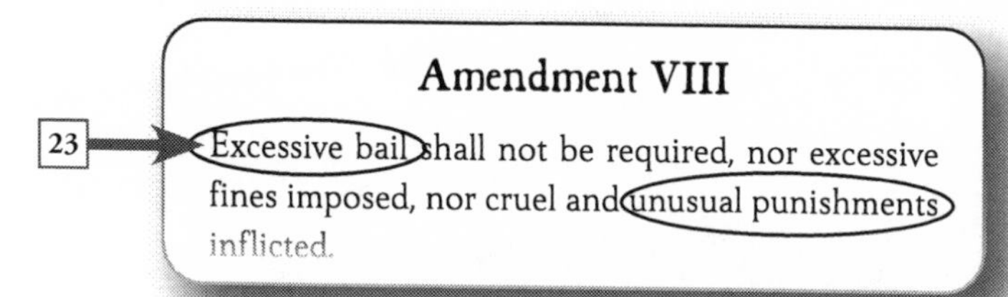
Amendment VIII

23 Excessive bail shall not be required, nor excessive fines imposed, nor cruel and unusual punishments inflicted.

Ninth Amendment.

24 All Rights Are Retained By the People

This catch-all provision gives Americans the right to claim any and all rights that belong to them whether or not they are mentioned in the Constitution. This Amendment prevents the government from violating a human right just because it is not in the Constitution or the Bill of Rights.

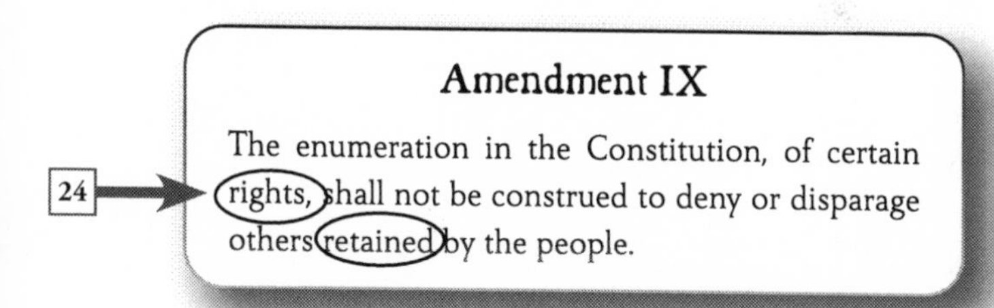
Amendment IX

24 The enumeration in the Constitution, of certain rights, shall not be construed to deny or disparage others retained by the people.

Tenth Amendment.

25 All Powers Not Delegated Are Retained By the People

While the Ninth Amendment declares that all human *rights* belong to the people, the Tenth Amendment gives all unassigned political *powers* to the states or the people.

25 →

Amendment X

The powers not delegated to the United States by the Constitution, nor prohibited by it to the States, are reserved to the States respectively, or to the people.

How Would You Decide?

The Supreme Court has been criticized for sidestepping the Ninth and Tenth Amendments when it ruled that some modern issues that were not listed in the Constitution were rightly a federal government responsibility. How would you decide? Put an X by who is best suited to deal with:

A state issue?		A federal issue?
____	Alcoholic drinks	____
____	Abortion	____
____	Marriage	____
____	Religion	____
____	Hate crimes	____
____	Illegal drugs	____
____	Police and fire	____
____	Food stamps	____
____	Education	____
____	Driver's license	____
____	Terrorist attacks	____
____	Hunting/fishing	____
____	Capital Punishment	____
____	Border Control	____

MEMORY TRICK

How to Remember the Bill of Rights

There's no simple trick like LEJ SASR to remember the Bill of Rights, but there are many ideas that will help if you take time to learn them.

The Number 27

First, you can remember the number of protected rights in the Bill of Rights because it's the same as the number of charges leveled at King George III (27), and the same number of Amendments to the Constitution (27). Most of the 27 protected rights may be memorized using the tricks shown below.

AMENDMENT I—Expression and Association

Trick: With one digit for #1 Amendment (your index finger), remember the five rights by pointing with your finger:

1. **Religion** (point to sky, toward God).
2. **Speech** (point to mouth).
3. **Press** (press finger on table or cell phone, get it?).
4. **Assembly** (make beckoning motion to beckon others to assemble).
5. **Petitioning** (write words in the air with finger).

AMENDMENT 2—Self Defense

Trick: With two digits for #2 Amendment (thumb and index finger), make the shape of a handgun.

AMENDMENT 3—Soldiers as House Guests

Trick: "Two's company, three's a crowd!" With three digits for #3 Amendment (first three fingers), remember you and your spouse (two) make a nice pair, but a soldier (third) is an unwanted crowd.

AMENDMENT 4—Illegal Search and Seizure

Trick: With four digits for #4 Amendment, make a fist. The four fingers are closed tightly on something to remind you of taking someone's property—seizing it.

AMENDMENT 5—Self-incrimination

Trick: Take all five digits for #5 Amendment and cover your mouth to remember that you cannot be forced to incriminate yourself.

*How to Remember the Details of Amendment 5—"Five to remember Five"

Trick: Call both hands your "Jury Hands" (many fingers = many jury members). To remember all five parts of the Fifth Amendment hold one Jury Hand high. All five digits stand for #5 Amendment.

1. **Grand jury hearing** (cup your Jury Hand to your ear so the jury may hear what you're charged with).
2. **No Forced Confessions** (grab your throat with your Jury Hand).
3. **No Two Trials for same Crime** (grab throat with *both* Jury Hands).
4 **Due Process** (put Jury Hands together, interlocking fingers. Court can't take life, liberty, or property without due process).
5. **Compensation** (hold hands in front of you in cupping shape—the court must pay you for property it takes).

AMENDMENT 6—Speedy and Public Trial

Trick: Hold out one hand and point to your wrist watch with the other. This brings to mind the right to a speedy trial.

**How to Remember the Details of Amendment 6—"Six to remember Six"

Trick: Holding out your Jury Hand raise one finger on the other hand to make 6 for #6 Amendment. Inside the court room are several individuals about whom this Amendment makes reference.

1. **Speedy Trial** (point to wristwatch).
2. **Charges** (the one finger is the judge who declares charges).

3. **Attorney** (the one finger is a lawyer assigned to represent you).
4. **Jury** (your Jury Hand represents your right to trial by jury).
5. **Witnesses against** (three fingers make a "W" to confront witnesses).
6. **Witnesses for** (three other fingers make a "W" to subpoena witnesses).

AMENDMENT 7—Jury Trial for $20 or more

Trick: Hold out your Jury Hand (counts as 5) and two other fingers for a total of seven for #7 Amendment. Make a fist with the five fingers to denote "zero." You are left looking at a 2 and a 0, standing for $20.

AMENDMENT 8—Cruel and Unusual Punishment

Trick: Raise both hands, curl your thumbs into your palm. The king has cruelly cut off your thumbs as punishment, leaving you only eight fingers for #8 Amendment.

AMENDMENT 9—Rights Not Listed

Trick: Show #9 Amendment by holding up both hands and displaying nine digits, hiding one of your thumbs in your palm. This brings to mind nine rights plain and clear to see, but one hidden from view that is just as real as the others—it represents unlisted rights.

AMENDMENT 10—Powers Not Listed

Trick: With both hands held open in front of you, and all ten digits representing all ten Amendments in the Bill of Rights, you have superpowers to lift the roof completely off of tyranny. Go ahead and lift it.

The 27 Protected Rights

1. Right to Religion
2. Right to Free Speech
3. Right to Free Press
4. Right to Assemble
5. Right to Petition
6. Right to Bear Arms
7. No Quartering of Troops
8. Secure in Persons, Papers, Effects
9. No Illegal Searches, Seizures
10. Must have Cause to Arrest
11. Charges Heard by Grand Jury
12. Grand Jury Hearing for Military except in a Court Martial
13. No Double Jeopardy
14. No Self-incrimination
15. Right to Due Process of law
16. Right to be Compensated
17. Right to Speedy trial
18. Right to Jury Trial
19. Right to Confront Witnesses
20. Right to Call Witnesses
21. Right to Defense Attorney
22. Right to Jury for Cases of $20+
23. Facts Remain on Appeal
24. No Excessive Bails, Fines
25. No Cruel, Unusual Punishments
26. Unspecified Rights are People's
27. Unspecified Powers are People's

TIMED READING

Read the Bill of Rights From Start to Finish

This exercise takes 10-15 minutes.

Materials Needed:

A red pen, pencil or highlighter, and a timer
A copy of the Bill of Rights (see page 164)

Underlining

As you read, underline 2-3 key words that bring to mind the meaning of a sentence or paragraph. Some good examples are those key words circled on the prior pages.

The Bill of Rights is very condensed, with many separate concepts in a single sentence (for help see the glossary). You may want to underline a lot of words. Instead, think of each Amendment as a short newspaper article. What would the headline be?

Timed Exercise

Start with the First Amendment and stop after you finish Amendment X.

Ready? Begin: Start the timer and begin reading.

Did you finish? Congratulations, you just read the Bill of Rights.

Time: ________ Date: __________________

TEST YOURSELF

Helpful Details

Now that you have a general understanding of the Bill of Rights, the answers to the following questions will not be difficult to find.

1. How many Amendments are in the Bill of Rights?

   ______

2. How many Amendments were first proposed? ______
3. How many Amendments were ratified? ______
4. Which is the longest Amendment? ______
5. Which is the shortest Amendment? ______
6. Opinion question: In your view what are the three most important rights protected in the Bill of Rights?

   a.

   b.

   c.

7. Which Amendment says the federal government is specifically restricted from exercising any power not granted to it by the states? _________

8. Which Amendment forbids the federal government from punishing you by cruel torture? _________

9. Which Amendment prevents the federal government from taking away farms from the farmers without buying the land from them? __________

10. Which Amendment restricts the federal government from interfering with the people's right to worship?

    ____

11. Can you think of two instances where the freedom of speech is correctly restricted and controlled?

    a.

    b.

12. Which Amendment prevents a person from being charged with a crime without first having a Grand Jury review the basis for the criminal charge?

    ____

13. Can you think of an instance when freedom of the press should be restricted and controlled?

    ____

* * * * *

Amendments 11-27

The following section briefly summarizes the remaining 17 Amendments.

It is remarkable that after more than 225 years in operation, the Constitution has required only 17 additional Amendments. This is a compliment to the brilliance and scholarship of the Framers' original version.

AMENDMENTS 11–27

11th Amendment—*Lawsuits*

The states cannot be sued by someone in another state without its consent.

12th Amendment—*Two Ballots in Electoral College*

This repaired how the Electoral College elects the President and Vice President (VP) using separate ballots.

13th Amendment—*No Slavery*

This abolished slavery except for criminals who are being punished.

14th Amendment—*Born in the USA*

People born in the United States are guaranteed the right to full citizenship.

15th Amendment—*Right to Vote*

The right to vote may not be denied because of someone's race, color or previous condition of servitude.

16th Amendment—*Income Tax*

The United States government is given the right to collect taxes on personal income.

17th Amendment—*Election of Senators*

The people are allowed to elect their Senators instead of having the state legislature appoint them.

18th Amendment—*No Alcoholic Drinks*

This abolished alcoholic liquors from being produced, transported, or sold.

19th Amendment—*Women's Vote*

This Amendment gave women the right to vote.

20th Amendment—*Date Change*

This shortened the waiting period of 13 months to 2 months before new Congressmen could be seated.

21st Amendment—*Alcoholic Drinks Allowed*

This repealed the Eighteenth Amendment giving the states sole power over alcoholic drinks.

22nd Amendment—*Two Terms*

This limited the president to two terms of office.

23rd Amendment—*D.C. Electors*

Washington D.C. residents were given the right to appoint Electors for presidential elections.

24th Amendment—*No Poll Tax To Vote*

The right to vote cannot be denied just because somebody is behind on paying his taxes.

25th Amendment—*Replacing President*

This Amendment describes how to replace the President or the VP if one dies or is removed from office.

26th Amendment—*18 Years Old May Vote*

Every American who turns 18 has the right to vote.

27th Amendment—*Congress's Pay Raises*

Senators and Congressmen can't accept a pay raise until after the next election. This makes it harder to vote themselves a raise.

ABOLISHING FREEDOM'S ENEMIES

With the first seating of Congress and President George Washington in 1789, the Framers successfully fulfilled a difficult task: they abolished all seven enemies of freedom, forever, on the condition that the Constitution remain intact, sustained, honored, and obeyed.

1. **Abolished the Ruler**: The framers prevented the rise of a king in America by diluting political power and spreading it among all the people. And, by carefully spelling out every governmental responsibility.
2. **Abolished Castes**: No one gets special treatment, but everyone can get representation in Congress.
3. **Abolished All Things in Common**: The framers called this "leveling," and abolished it by protecting the right to acquire property, develop it, and sell it for profit.
4. **Minimal Regulation**: This power was given to Congress who had to be answerable to the voters.

5. **Limited Governmental Force**: The power to compel and coerce to maintain justice and order is controlled by the people themselves, with help from a court system.
6. **Information Flow**: The right to information is guaranteed by freedom of speech, press, petition and association—and obligatory governmental reports.
7. **Rights**: The Framers guaranteed unalienable rights by granting to the federal government no more rights than those held by the people themselves: "If I can't do it then neither can they!"

FREEDOM IS
THE PEOPLE'S POWER TO EXERCISE
THEIR UNALIENABLE RIGHTS
AND TO CONTROL AND CHANGE
THEIR GOVERNMENT

PART V

PREAMBLE & THE SEVEN ARTICLES MADE EASIER

THE PREAMBLE

The Framer's Statement of Purpose

Now that you have read the Preamble and the seven Articles for a general overview, this exercise will help you pull out the main messages from each.

A wise man once said, "You'll never hear the answers if you don't ask the questions."

The Constitution is loaded with answers that most people miss because they are not asking questions. What follows are some questions to help trigger that process of exploration and discovery.

Standing at the very head of the Constitution are some goals the Framers expected all government activities to promote. Those goals are listed in a short introductory statement called the Preamble.

TEST YOURSELF

Helpful Details

Read the Preamble to the Constitution and answer the following questions (see page 145).

1. According to the first three words, to whom does all national authority belong? ______________________

2. From the Preamble how many individual objectives do We the People hope to achieve? _______

3. List the Preamble's main objectives here:

   a.

   b.

   c.

   d.

   e.

   f.

4. Who are the parties that the Constitution was designed to more perfectly unite in a "more perfect Union"? ______________________________

5. Every American has his life and liberty protected equally. This is the positive outcome of establishing equal justice. What is an example of un-equal protection or unequal justice?

   a.

6. Who do Americans rely on to maintain peace, security and "domestic tranquility"

   a. on the national level? ____________________

   b. on the local level? ______________________

7. George Washington, Benjamin Franklin, and others said that the way to secure peace and provide for the Common Defense was to be prepared for war always. With whom is America "prepared for war always?"

   Name two external enemies:

   a.

   b.

   Name two internal enemies:

   c.

   d.

8. The Preamble's phrase "promote the general welfare" refers to spending the nation's resources on the well-being of the entire nation. Can you name two examples? Two have been already been provided.
   a. A strong, well-developed military
   b. A legal system for protecting copyrights, patents
   c.
   d.

9. Blessings of liberty: Sam Adams said "But neither the wisest constitution nor the wisest laws will secure the liberty and happiness of a people whose manners are universally corrupt." Are Americans losing liberties? Are Americans "corrupted"? Explain.

MEMORY TRICK

How to Remember the Preamble

A good reason to learn and remember the Preamble is because it summarizes the six goals that the Constitution promises to achieve. Do you believe all six promises are still intact in America today? Use the Preamble to find out. Here's how to remember it.

START—WE THE PEOPLE

Trick: Hold up your left hand, fingers spread wide. All those fingers represent "We the People."

PROMISE #1—FORM a more PERFECT UNION

Trick: Close your hand and make a fist as if forming clay in your palm.

Trick: With your fist closed point to where a wedding ring goes to make your "perfect union." The ring goes on your finger "in order to form a more perfect union."

PROMISE #2—Establish JUSTICE

Trick: Was it a legal marriage? Was it performed by a justice of the peace? Open your fist to a cupping shape to make one side of the scales of justice. Bring up your other cupped hand to create the pair, "to establish justice."

(Hint: if you forget the word "establish," then before opening your left fist look at it sideways. Notice how the fingers curled down and the thumb curled up make an "e" for "establish"?)

PROMISE #3—Insure domestic TRANQUILITY

Trick: Yes, your union *is* legal! Now you may rest in peace by bringing both hands, palms together, under your head as if on your pillow at home, because you have ensured "domestic tranquility."

PROMISE #4—Provide common DEFENSE

Trick: As you sleep in domestic tranquility, suddenly you hear the glass break—a burglar is trying to get in. Make two fists and "provide for the common defense."

PROMISE #5—Promote the general WELFARE

Trick: The burglary was a false alarm—the TV was left on. Relax your fists and open them, palms up. Do you see three fingers on each hand making a "W"? That makes you want to promote the "general welfare."

PROMISE #6a—Secure blessings of LIBERTY

Trick: Clasp your two hands with fingers interlocking as if praying, and hold secure between them your blessings. Your upright thumbs remind you there's an "L" in blessing, and an "L" in Liberty, "to secure the blessings of liberty."

PROMISE #6b—To ourselves and our POSTERITY

Trick: Bring your two hands to your heart then drop them to reach for your children. The valuable significance here is that the Framers intended this Constitution to last for the ages—for "ourselves and our Posterity."

ARTICLE I

The Legislative Branch

The Framers considered the power to make laws to be the most important part of the government. They gave the job to Congress and made it the central power plant for the entire system. They also didn't want Congress to become a supreme power unto itself. They chained it down with lists of powers and restraints, and built-in checks and balances. They also restricted the states so they couldn't complicate this new system. Please read Article I to answer the following questions.

SECTION 1

1. Who has all law-making powers? ______________

2. Name the two "houses" in the Legislative Branch

    a.

    b.

SECTION 2

1. How long is the term for a Representative? _______

2. At what age may you be a Representative? _______

3. Which House has sole power to impeach? _______

SECTION 3

1. How long is the term for a Senator? _______

2. At what age may you be a Senator? _______

3. How much of the Senate is replaced every two years?

   ____

4. Which House has sole power to put impeachments on trial? ___________________________

5. What's the worst punishment an impeached official can receive from the Senate?

   ____

SECTION 4

1. Is Congress permitted to force the states to hold elections on a certain day? _______

SECTION 5

1. Is Congress permitted to force members to attend sessions? ____

2. What must each House obtain before adjourning for more than three days while the Congress is in Session? ___________________________

SECTION 6

1. May a Congressman be arrested for minor offenses while Congress is in session? _______

2. May a sitting Congressman hold other offices in the government at the same time? _______

SECTION 7

1. Which House has direct responsibility for and supervision over raising taxes?

   ____

2. What portion of the two Houses of Congress is needed to pass a bill into law that the President has vetoed (rejected)?

   ____

SECTION 8

This Section is critically important. It lists the 20 powers granted to Congress. Many of these powers are vulnerable to misuse so the Framers put into the Constitution several necessary and helpful protections so the people would not lose their rights. This invention is known as the Framers' constitutional system of checks and balances.

For each Clause, find the main power and list it here. A few have already been done for you.

1. Clause 1, power to tax
2. Clause 1, power to spend

3. Clause 2,
4. Clause 3,
5. Clause 4, make the rules for citizenship
6. Clause 4, make the bankruptcy laws
7. Clause 5,
8. Clause 5,
9. Clause 6,
10. Clause 7,
11. Clause 8,
12. Clause 9,
13. Clause 10,
14. Clause 11,
15. Clause 12 & 13, Raise and finance the military
16. Clause 14,
17. Clause 15 & 16, Call up state militias
18. Clause 17, Administer the seat of government
19. Clause 17, Administer federal lands
20. Clause 18,

SECTION 9

This Section may represent the first time in history that restraints have been put on a legislative body. There have been curbs put on kings, rulers, and presidents, but never on the legislature in this fashion. There are eight major restraints in Section 9. Please list them here. A few have already been done for you.

1. Clause 1, Congress can't stop slave importations
2. Clause 2,

3. Clause 3,
4. Clause 4, no capitation or direct taxes
5. Clause 5, no tax or duty on states' exports
6. Clause 6,
7. Clause 7,
8. Clause 8, no aristocratic titles of nobility allowed

SECTION 10

As shown above, Article 1 Section 8 outlines the powers that were granted to the federal government. The Framers used Section 10 to make it clear that the powers the states once had are now transferred and they could no longer exercise them. Section 10 puts chains on the states in one of two ways. Clause 1 lists activities that are absolutely prohibited. Clauses 2 and 3 list what the states may do if they first obtain permission from Congress.

1. Clause 1: Please list the nine activities that the states may not do. A few have already been done for you.
    1. Enter into treaties
    2.
    3.
    4.
    5.
    6. No Bill of Attainder (people can't be declared outlaws by legislative enactment, only by a fair trial)

7.
8. No new laws allowed that will hurt existing contracts
9.

2. Clause 2: Is one state permitted to charge another state a fee for selling their product across their state line? ________

3. Clause 3: Is a state permitted to fight a war with another nation? ____________. Under what conditions is that restriction set aside?

____

ARTICLE II

The Executive Branch

It was the original intent of the Framers to carefully limit the powers of the federal government, in particular, the office of president. Today, the presidency has become the most powerful political office in the world. It remains the role of Congress and the Judiciary to serve as a check and balance, and to prevent a president from expanding that power beyond the boundaries set by the Constitution.

SECTION 1

1. Clause 1: How long is the President's term of office?

   ____

2. Clause 1: Who has the job of enforcing the laws passed by Congress? ____________________________

3. Clause 2: How many Electors may each state name to formally elect the President?

   ____

4. Clause 3: Who decides on what day to hold the elections for President? ______________________

5. Clause 4: May a foreigner who has permanently settled in America hold the office of President?

   ______

SECTION 2

1. The President is in charge of what two defenses?

   ________________ ________________

2. Clause 2: May the President make a treaty without the consent of the Senate? ______

SECTION 3

1. Is the President required to give a State of the Union report to Congress? ______

2. May the President lawfully ignore a law passed by Congress and not "faithfully execute" it? ______

SECTION 4

1. What are three reasons a President may be removed from office? ______________ ______________

   ____

Six Areas of Constitutional Responsibility

In summary, the President's constitutional duties are limited to six areas of responsibility.

- Chief of State over 320 million Americans.
- Commander in Chief over a military force of about two million active and reserve personnel.
- Chief Executive Officer of the Executive Branch.
- Chief diplomat for handling foreign relations.
- Chief architect for needed legislation.
- The conscience of the nation in granting pardons and reprieves when he feels justice requires them.

To this list Congress has added dozens of additional responsibilities to the Executive Branch that involve many regulatory agencies with budgets totaling hundreds of billions of dollars.

ARTICLE III

The Judicial Branch

The Supreme Court is the guardian of the Constitution. This means it can review new laws to make certain they don't violate the provisions set forth in the Constitution.

An impartial court system is crucial to the success of self-government. It plays a vital role in the Framers' system of checks and balances.

SECTION 1

1. The Constitution established the Supreme Court. Whose job is it to establish the lower courts across America? ______________________________

2. So long as judges serve with "good behavior," how long may they hold that office? __________________

SECTION 2

1. Clauses 1 & 2: If the people have a question concerning the Constitution, may they bring it to the federal courts to decide? _______

2. Clauses 1 & 2: List four examples of cases the federal courts are made responsible to look at:
   a.
   b.
   c.
   d.

3. Clause 3: The trials of all crimes shall be by jury except for: ________________________

4. Clause 3: Why do you think it is important that the accused be tried for his crime in the same state where the crime was committed? (Hint: think about travel, witnesses, expenses)

SECTION 3

1. Clause 1: Treason is the only crime that is specifically defined in the Constitution. List its two offenses.

   a.

   b.

2. Clause 1: How many witnesses to the act of treason must exist for a conviction? _______

3. Clause 2: Who has the power to decide what the punishment will be for treason? _________________

ARTICLE IV

The States

The Framers' first great task was to control the federal government. They achieved this by creating three branches of government and balancing them carefully so they would work together with checks against abuses. The next great task was to get the states to cooperate together. The Framers achieved this with several "nationalizing" rules that made the states individually strong, yet unified in their common causes as truly united states.

For more information about how territories were initially organized and prepared to become states, see the Northwest Ordinance, passed by Congress in 1787.

SECTION 1

1. Must each of the states recognize the official acts of all the other states? _______

2. Give three examples of official acts that are recognized among the states (one is already provided).
   a. Marriage licenses

b.

c.

SECTION 2

1. Clause 1: A driver using a valid driver's license in another state is an example of being entitled to the same privilege or immunity (circle one) of citizens in the several states. (See glossary)

2. Clause 2: May a fugitive from justice find sanctuary from capture in another state? _______. An interesting side note: If a governor believes a fugitive hiding in his state will not receive fair and humane treatment if the criminal is sent back, the governor may refuse to release (extradite) him. The language in the Constitution makes it sound as though the fugitive's return is mandatory upon request, but the Supreme Court has held that the courts cannot force a governor to extradite.

SECTION 3

1. Clause 1: May new states be admitted? _______

2. Clause 1: May a new state be created inside an existing state without approval of the state legislature?

   ____

3. Clause 1: May two states, or parts of states, be joined together to make one state without agreement from their respective legislatures? _______

4. Clause 2: Who has sole power to dispose of territory and property belonging to the United States?__________________ Interesting side note: When President Jimmy Carter gave away the Panama Canal, many believed he violated Article 4 Section 3 of the Constitution because he did so without consent of the House.

SECTION 4

1. What form of government does the U.S. guarantee to every state? ______________________________

2. What does "Republican Form" mean? (See glossary)

   ____

ARTICLE V

Amending the Constitution

James Madison said the Framers hoped their successors would "improve and perpetuate" the Constitution. However, they were concerned that their polished formula for a divided, balanced, and limited government could be mutilated by careless or rash meddling. For that reason the process for changing the Constitution was made cumbersome and thorough. This was meant to prevent the random tides of popular opinion from smothering eternal principles of liberty.

CLAUSE 1

1. May the American people change their Constitution?

   ____

2. How many members of the House and Senate must approve a proposed Amendment? _______

3. How many state legislatures must ratify (approve) a proposed Amendment for it to become law? _______

4. If Congress refuses to consider an Amendment, may the states gather and propose Amendments? ________

5. How many states must agree to hold a Constitutional Convention to propose an Amendment? ________

6. Do Amendments passed in a Constitutional Convention automatically become law? ________

7. How many states must ratify an Amendment approved in a Constitutional Convention to make it law? ______

ARTICLE VI

Supremacy of the Constitution, Debts, Oaths

The Framers wanted to assure banks and creditors that their new government would honor all of the debts incurred during the War for Independence. They also wanted to put in writing the clarification of the supremacy of the Constitution, the federal treaties, and the federal laws over state constitutions and state laws.

1. Clause 1: How many debts and obligations was the new American government willing to pay back in full?

   ____

2. Clause 2: What document is the supreme law of the land? ____

3. Clause 3: At the time the Constitution was adopted there were many Americans who had a much stronger sense of loyalty toward their own states than toward the Union. What did the Framers require of every federal officer as

a reminder that their first loyalty was now to the federal Constitution? ________________________________

4. Clause 3: May an American be required to pass a religious test to hold federal office? _______

ARTICLE VII

Ratification

One of the biggest stumbling blocks with the Articles of Confederation was the requirement that all 13 states be in favor of a decision before any action could be taken. That meant any single state had the power to upset all the other states' hard work by simply voting "No." That policy created so much backlog, nothing was getting done, and there was a war to be fought.

The Framers decided that unanimous support for ratification was too difficult to achieve in a timely fashion. They didn't want the impediments and limitations from the war years to repeat themselves.

For that reason they made ratification of the Constitution possible with just a super-majority vote. It was formally agreed that only nine states would be needed to make the Constitution the law of the land.

CLAUSE 1

1. How many states must ratify the Constitution for it to become law? _______

2. Last Paragraph: On what date was the Constitution finished and signed by the Framers?

   ____

PART VI

HISTORICAL BASICS

HISTORICAL BASICS
Of the Constitution

Purpose: To provide for the common defense, protect human rights, establish a representative form of government.

Framers: Delegates from the original thirteen states

Parchment: Four sheets 28-3/4 in. by 23-5/8 in. each

Words: 4,379 (4,609 including signatures, etc.)
7,591 including the 27 amendments

Articles: 7

Amendments: 27

Constitutional Convention: May 25 - September 17, 1787, in the Pennsylvania State House, now Independence Hall

Signers: 55 total signers, 55 total delegates
42 delegates usually attended the Convention
39 delegates actually signed on September 17, 1787
3 delegates did not sign until there was a bill of rights

Nine States to Ratify:

Delaware—December 7, 1787

Pennsylvania—December 12, 1787

New Jersey—December 18, 1787

Georgia—January 2, 1788

Connecticut—January 9, 1788

Massachusetts—February 6, 1788

Maryland—April 28, 1788

South Carolina—May 23, 1788

New Hampshire—June 21, 1788

Constitution is officially established on June 21, 1788

Remaining states that joined afterward: Virginia (June 25, 1788), New York (July 26, 1788), North Carolina (November 21, 1789), Rhode Island (May 29, 1790)

Time to Ratify: 9 months from signing to ninth state ratifying

Signed: September 17, 1787

Ratified: June 21, 1788

First Congress seated: March 4, 1789

First President seated: George Washington, April 30, 1789

Supreme Court convenes: February 2, 1790

Second President seated: John Adams, March 4, 1797

IMPORTANT DATES

April 19, 1775: Battle of Lexington, War for Independence starts.

July 4, 1776: Declaration of Independence adopted by Congress.

November 15, 1777: Articles of Confederation created.

March 1, 1781: Articles of Confederation ratified.

October 19, 1781: Cornwallis surrenders at Yorktown, ending British military action and the war.

September 3, 1783: Treaty of Paris signed. Great Britain recognizes colonists' independence.

May 25, 1787: The Constitutional Convention opens in Philadelphia to discuss revising the Articles of Confederation.

July 13, 1787: Congress passes the Northwest Ordinance.

September 17, 1787: All 12 state delegations approve the Constitution and the Convention formally adjourns.

June 21, 1788: The Constitution becomes effective for the ratifying states when New Hampshire is the 9th state to ratify.

March 4, 1789: The first Congress under the Constitution convenes in New York City.

April 30, 1789: George Washington is inaugurated as the first president of the United States.

June 8, 1789: James Madison introduced proposed Bill of Rights in the House of Representatives.

September 24, 1789: Congress establishes a Supreme Court, 13 district courts, three ad hoc circuit courts, and the position of Attorney General.

September 25, 1789: Congress approves 12 Amendments and sends them to the states for ratification.

February 2, 1790: Supreme Court convenes for the first time after an unsuccessful attempt February 1.

December 15, 1791: Virginia ratifies the Bill of Rights, and 10 of the 12 proposed Amendments become part of the Constitution.

MAKE IT A HABIT

The key to remembering how freedom works in America is to frequently shine the light of the Constitution and the Declaration upon the actions of politicians. That is the best way to make sure individual human rights are being respected according to the promises in America's two founding documents.

Select Two Days Each Year

Many millions of Americans will choose a specific day each year to re-read these documents from start to finish. As we learned in the prior pages it does not take a great deal of time, even when reading them aloud.

July 4th is a good day to read the Declaration of Independence. It was on that day in 1776 that the Framers put their lives, their fortunes, and their sacred honor in serious jeopardy when they signed that document in Independence Hall in Philadelphia, Pennsylvania.

September 17th is a good day to read the Constitution from start to finish. It was on that day in 1787 that America's grand experiment in self-government and liberty was born, an important birthday worth celebrating by all people everywhere seeking freedom and liberty.

PART VII

THE DECLARATION OF INDEPENDENCE & THE CONSTITUTION

TEXT

The text of the Declaration of Independence and the Constitution is copied from transcripts available at the official website of the National Archives: www.archives.gov.

GLOSSARY

If you encounter a word that doesn't make sense, go to page 179 for a glossary of terms. Many of the words in the Declaration and Constitution have more than one meaning. The glossary provides the meaning intended for these documents.

To learn about other definitions used by Americans in the late 1700s, see Noah Webster's American Dictionary of the English Language, published in 1828. That book has been reprinted and is now available.

EASY-REFERENCE LINE NUMBERS

Do you need a way to quickly direct someone's attention to a specific line of text in the Declaration or Constitution? For your convenience, a column of numbers is printed on the outside margins of each page. You can use these numbers, along with page numbers, to help readers find things fast.

The Declaration of Independence

IN CONGRESS, July 4, 1776.

The unanimous Declaration of the thirteen United States of America

When in the Course of human events, it becomes necessary for one people to dissolve the political bands which have connected them with another, and to assume among the powers of the earth, the separate and equal station to which the Laws of Nature and of Nature's God entitle them, a decent respect to the opinions of mankind requires that they should declare the causes which impel them to the separation. 1 5

We hold these truths to be self-evident, that all men are created equal, that they are endowed by their Creator with certain unalienable Rights, that among these are Life, Liberty and the pursuit of Happiness.—That to secure these rights, Governments are instituted among Men, deriving their just powers from the consent of the governed, —That whenever any Form of Government becomes destructive of these ends, it is the Right of the People to alter or to abolish it, and to institute new Government, laying its foundation on such principles and organizing its powers in such form, as to them shall seem most likely to effect their 10 15 20

Safety and Happiness. Prudence, indeed, will dictate that Governments long established should not be changed for light and transient causes; and accordingly all experience hath shewn, that mankind are more disposed to suffer, while evils are sufferable, than to right themselves by abolishing the forms to which they are accustomed. But when a long train of abuses and usurpations, pursuing invariably the same Object evinces a design to reduce them under absolute Despotism, it is their right, it is their duty, to throw off such Government, and to provide new Guards for their future security.—Such has been the patient sufferance of these Colonies; and such is now the necessity which constrains them to alter their former Systems of Government. The history of the present King of Great Britain is a history of repeated injuries and usurpations, all having in direct object the establishment of an absolute Tyranny over these States. To prove this, let Facts be submitted to a candid world.

He has refused his Assent to Laws, the most wholesome and necessary for the public good.

He has forbidden his Governors to pass Laws of immediate and pressing importance, unless suspended in their operation till his Assent should be obtained; and when so suspended, he has utterly neglected to attend to them.

He has refused to pass other Laws for the accommodation of large districts of people, unless those people would relinquish the right of Representation in the Legislature, a right inestimable to them and formidable to tyrants only.

HE has called together legislative bodies at places unusual, uncomfortable, and distant from the depository of their public Records, for the sole purpose of fatiguing them into compliance with his measures. 1

HE has dissolved Representative Houses repeatedly, for opposing with manly firmness his invasions on the rights of the people. 5

HE has refused for a long time, after such dissolutions, to cause others to be elected; whereby the Legislative powers, incapable of Annihilation, have returned to the People at large for their exercise; the State remaining in the mean time exposed to all the dangers of invasion from without, and convulsions within. 10

HE has endeavoured to prevent the population of these States; for that purpose obstructing the Laws for Naturalization of Foreigners; refusing to pass others to encourage their migrations hither, and raising the conditions of new Appropriations of Lands. 15 20

HE has obstructed the Administration of Justice, by refusing his Assent to Laws for establishing Judiciary powers.

HE has made Judges dependent on his Will alone, for the tenure of their offices, and the amount and payment of their salaries. 25

HE has erected a multitude of New Offices, and sent hither swarms of Officers to harass our people, and eat out their substance.

HE has kept among us, in times of peace, Standing Armies without the Consent of our legislatures. 30

1 HE has affected to render the Military independent of and superior to the Civil power.

HE has combined with others to subject us to a jurisdiction foreign to our constitution, and
5 unacknowledged by our laws; giving his Assent to their Acts of pretended Legislation:

FOR Quartering large bodies of armed troops among us:

FOR protecting them, by a mock Trial, from
10 punishment for any Murders which they should commit on the Inhabitants of these States:

FOR cutting off our Trade with all parts of the world:

FOR imposing Taxes on us without our Consent:

15 FOR depriving us in many cases, of the benefits of Trial by Jury:

FOR transporting us beyond Seas to be tried for pretended offences:

FOR abolishing the free System of English Laws
20 in a neighboring Province, establishing therein an Arbitrary government, and enlarging its Boundaries so as to render it at once an example and fit instrument for introducing the same absolute rule into these Colonies:

25 FOR taking away our Charters, abolishing our most valuable Laws, and altering fundamentally the Forms of our Governments:

FOR suspending our own Legislatures, and declaring themselves invested with power to legislate
30 for us in all cases whatsoever.

HE has abdicated Government here, by declaring us out of his Protection and waging War against us.

He has plundered our seas, ravaged our Coasts, burnt our towns, and destroyed the lives of our people.

He is at this time transporting large Armies of foreign Mercenaries to compleat the works of death, desolation and tyranny, already begun with circumstances of Cruelty & perfidy scarcely paralleled in the most barbarous ages, and totally unworthy the Head of a civilized nation.

He has constrained our fellow Citizens taken Captive on the high Seas to bear Arms against their Country, to become the executioners of their friends and Brethren, or to fall themselves by their Hands.

He has excited domestic insurrections amongst us, and has endeavoured to bring on the inhabitants of our frontiers, the merciless Indian Savages, whose known rule of warfare, is an undistinguished destruction of all ages, sexes and conditions.

In every stage of these Oppressions We have Petitioned for Redress in the most humble terms: Our repeated Petitions have been answered only by repeated injury. A Prince whose character is thus marked by every act which may define a Tyrant, is unfit to be the ruler of a free people.

Nor have We been wanting in attentions to our British brethren. We have warned them from time to time of attempts by their legislature to extend an unwarrantable jurisdiction over us. We have reminded them of the circumstances of our emigration and settlement here. We have appealed to their native justice and magnanimity, and we have conjured them by the ties of our common kindred to

1 disavow these usurpations, which, would inevitably interrupt our connections and correspondence. They too have been deaf to the voice of justice and of consanguinity. We must, therefore, acquiesce in 5 the necessity, which denounces our Separation, and hold them, as we hold the rest of mankind, Enemies in War, in Peace Friends.

We, therefore, the Representatives of the UNITED STATES OF AMERICA, in General 10 Congress, Assembled, appealing to the Supreme Judge of the world for the rectitude of our intentions, do, in the Name, and by Authority of the good People of these Colonies, solemnly publish and declare, That these United Colonies are, and of Right ought 15 to be Free and Independent States; that they are Absolved from all Allegiance to the British Crown, and that all political connection between them and the State of Great Britain, is and ought to be totally dissolved; and that as Free and Independent 20 States, they have full Power to levy War, conclude Peace, contract Alliances, establish Commerce, and to do all other Acts and Things which Independent States may of right do. And for the support of this Declaration, with a firm reliance on the protection of 25 divine Providence, we mutually pledge to each other our Lives, our Fortunes and our sacred Honor.

The 56 signatures on the Declaration of Independence (In the order that they appear on the document)

Georgia:
- Button Gwinnett
- Lyman Hall
- George Walton

North Carolina:
- William Hooper
- Joseph Hewes
- John Penn

South Carolina:
- Edward Rutledge
- Thomas Heyward, Jr.
- Thomas Lynch, Jr.
- Arthur Middleton

Massachusetts:
- John Hancock

Maryland:
- Samuel Chase
- William Paca
- Thomas Stone
- Charles Carroll of Carrollton

Virginia:
- George Wythe
- Richard Henry Lee
- Thomas Jefferson
- Benjamin Harrison
- Thomas Nelson, Jr.
- Francis Lightfoot Lee
- Carter Braxton

Pennsylvania:
- Robert Morris
- Benjamin Rush
- Benjamin Franklin
- John Morton
- George Clymer
- James Smith
- George Taylor
- James Wilson
- George Ross

Delaware:
- Caesar Rodney
- George Read
- Thomas McKean

New York:
- William Floyd
- Philip Livingston
- Francis Lewis
- Lewis Morris

New Jersey:
- Richard Stockton
- John Witherspoon
- Francis Hopkinson
- John Hart
- Abraham Clark

New Hampshire:

Josiah Bartlett

William Whipple

Massachusetts:

Samuel Adams

John Adams

Robert Treat Paine

Elbridge Gerry

Rhode Island:

Stephen Hopkins

William Ellery

Connecticut:

Roger Sherman

Samuel Huntington

William Williams

Oliver Wolcott

New Hampshire:

Matthew Thornton

CONSTITUTION OF THE UNITED STATES

We the People of the United States, in Order to form a more perfect Union, establish Justice, insure domestic Tranquility, provide for the common defence, promote the general Welfare, and secure the Blessings of Liberty to ourselves and our Posterity, do ordain and establish this Constitution for the United States of America.

Article I.

SECTION 1. All legislative Powers herein granted shall be vested in a Congress of the United States, which shall consist of a Senate and House of Representatives.

SECTION 2. The House of Representatives shall be composed of Members chosen every second Year by the People of the several States, and the Electors in each State shall have the Qualifications requisite for Electors of the most numerous Branch of the State Legislature.

No Person shall be a Representative who shall not have attained to the Age of twenty five Years, and been seven Years a Citizen of the United States, and who shall not, when elected, be an Inhabitant of that State in which he shall be chosen.

1 [Representatives and direct Taxes shall be apportioned among the several States which may be included within this Union, according to their respective Numbers, which shall be determined
5 by adding to the whole Number of free Persons, including those bound to Service for a Term of Years, and excluding Indians not taxed, three fifths of all other Persons.][1] The actual Enumeration shall be made within three Years after the first
10 Meeting of the Congress of the United States, and within every subsequent Term of ten Years, in such Manner as they shall by Law direct. The Number of Representatives shall not exceed one for every thirty Thousand, but each State shall have at Least
15 one Representative; and until such enumeration shall be made, the State of New Hampshire shall be entitled to choose three, Massachusetts eight, Rhode Island and Providence Plantations one, Connecticut five, New York six, New Jersey
20 four, Pennsylvania eight, Delaware one, Maryland six, Virginia ten, North Carolina five, South Carolina five and Georgia three.

When vacancies happen in the Representation from any State, the Executive Authority thereof shall
25 issue Writs of Election to fill such Vacancies.

The House of Representatives shall choose their Speaker and other Officers; and shall have the sole Power of Impeachment.

SECTION 3. The Senate of the United States
30 shall be composed of two Senators from each State, [chosen by the Legislature thereof,][2] for six Years; and each Senator shall have one Vote.

1 Changed by section 2 of the Fourteenth Amendment.

2 Changed by the Seventeenth Amendment.

Immediately after they shall be assembled in Consequence of the first Election, they shall be divided as equally as may be into three Classes. The Seats of the Senators of the first Class shall be vacated at the Expiration of the second Year, of the second Class at the Expiration of the fourth Year, and of the third Class at the Expiration of the sixth Year, so that one third may be chosen every second Year; [and if Vacancies happen by Resignation, or otherwise, during the Recess of the Legislature of any State, the Executive thereof may make temporary Appointments until the next Meeting of the Legislature, which shall then fill such Vacancies.][3] 1 5 10

No person shall be a Senator who shall not have attained to the Age of thirty Years, and been nine Years a Citizen of the United States, and who shall not, when elected, be an Inhabitant of that State for which he shall be chosen. 15

The Vice President of the United States shall be President of the Senate, but shall have no Vote, unless they be equally divided. 20

The Senate shall choose their other Officers, and also a President pro tempore, in the absence of the Vice President, or when he shall exercise the Office of President of the United States. 25

The Senate shall have the sole Power to try all Impeachments. When sitting for that Purpose, they shall be on Oath or Affirmation. When the President of the United States is tried, the Chief Justice shall preside: And no Person shall be convicted without the Concurrence of two thirds of the Members present. 30

Judgment in Cases of Impeachment shall not extend further than to removal from Office, and 34

3 Changed by the Seventeenth Amendment.

disqualification to hold and enjoy any Office of honor, Trust or Profit under the United States: but the Party convicted shall nevertheless be liable and subject to Indictment, Trial, Judgment and Punishment, according to Law.

SECTION 4. The Times, Places and Manner of holding Elections for Senators and Representatives, shall be prescribed in each State by the Legislature thereof; but the Congress may at any time by Law make or alter such Regulations, except as to the Place of Choosing Senators.

The Congress shall assemble at least once in every Year, and such Meeting shall be [on the first Monday in December,][4] unless they shall by Law appoint a different Day.

SECTION 5. Each House shall be the Judge of the Elections, Returns and Qualifications of its own Members, and a Majority of each shall constitute a Quorum to do Business; but a smaller number may adjourn from day to day, and may be authorized to compel the Attendance of absent Members, in such Manner, and under such Penalties as each House may provide.

Each House may determine the Rules of its Proceedings, punish its Members for disorderly Behavior, and, with the Concurrence of two-thirds, expel a Member.

Each House shall keep a Journal of its Proceedings, and from time to time publish the same, excepting such Parts as may in their Judgment require Secrecy; and the Yeas and Nays of the Members of either House on any question shall, at the Desire of one fifth of those Present, be entered on the Journal.

---

4 Changed by Section 2 of the Twentieth Amendment.

Neither House, during the Session of Congress, shall, without the Consent of the other, adjourn for more than three days, nor to any other Place than that in which the two Houses shall be sitting.

SECTION 6. The Senators and Representatives shall receive a Compensation for their Services, to be ascertained by Law, and paid out of the Treasury of the United States. They shall in all Cases, except Treason, Felony and Breach of the Peace, be privileged from Arrest during their Attendance at the Session of their respective Houses, and in going to and returning from the same; and for any Speech or Debate in either House, they shall not be questioned in any other Place.

No Senator or Representative shall, during the Time for which he was elected, be appointed to any civil Office under the Authority of the United States which shall have been created, or the Emoluments whereof shall have been increased during such time; and no Person holding any Office under the United States, shall be a Member of either House during his Continuance in Office.

SECTION 7. All bills for raising Revenue shall originate in the House of Representatives; but the Senate may propose or concur with Amendments as on other Bills.

Every Bill which shall have passed the House of Representatives and the Senate, shall, before it become a Law, be presented to the President of the United States; If he approve he shall sign it, but if not he shall return it, with his Objections to that House in which it shall have originated, who shall enter the Objections at large on their Journal, and proceed to reconsider it. If after such Reconsideration two thirds of that House shall agree to pass the Bill, it shall be sent, together with the Objections, to the other House, by which it shall likewise be reconsidered, and if approved by two thirds of that House, it shall become a Law. But in all such Cases the Votes of both Houses shall be determined by Yeas and Nays, and the Names of the Persons voting for and against the Bill shall be entered on the Journal of each House respectively. If any Bill shall not be returned by the President within ten Days (Sundays excepted) after it shall have been presented to him, the Same shall be a Law, in like Manner as if he had signed it, unless the Congress by their Adjournment prevent its Return, in which Case it shall not be a Law.

Every Order, Resolution, or Vote to which the Concurrence of the Senate and House of Representatives may be necessary (except on a question of Adjournment) shall be presented to the President of the United States; and before the Same shall take Effect, shall be approved by him, or being disapproved by him, shall be repassed by two thirds of the Senate and House of Representatives, according to the Rules and Limitations prescribed in the Case of a Bill.

SECTION 8. The Congress shall have Power To lay and collect Taxes, Duties, Imposts and Excises, to pay the Debts and provide for the common Defence and general Welfare of the United States; but all Duties, Imposts and Excises shall be uniform throughout the United States;

To borrow money on the credit of the United States;

To regulate Commerce with foreign Nations, and among the several States, and with the Indian Tribes;

To establish an uniform Rule of Naturalization, and uniform Laws on the subject of Bankruptcies throughout the United States;

To coin Money, regulate the Value thereof, and of foreign Coin, and fix the Standard of Weights and Measures;

To provide for the Punishment of counterfeiting the Securities and current Coin of the United States;

To establish Post Offices and Post Roads;

To promote the Progress of Science and useful Arts, by securing for limited Times to Authors and Inventors the exclusive Right to their respective Writings and Discoveries;

To constitute Tribunals inferior to the supreme Court;

To define and punish Piracies and Felonies committed on the high Seas, and Offenses against the Law of Nations;

To declare War, grant Letters of Marque and Reprisal, and make Rules concerning Captures on Land and Water;

To raise and support Armies, but no Appropriation of Money to that Use shall be for a longer Term than two Years;

To provide and maintain a Navy;

To make Rules for the Government and Regulation of the land and naval Forces;

To provide for calling forth the Militia to execute the Laws of the Union, suppress Insurrections and repel Invasions;

To provide for organizing, arming, and disciplining, the Militia, and for governing such Part of them as may be employed in the Service of the United States, reserving to the States respectively, the Appointment of the Officers, and the Authority

1 of training the Militia according to the discipline prescribed by Congress;

To exercise exclusive Legislation in all Cases whatsoever, over such District (not exceeding 5 ten Miles square) as may, by Cession of particular States, and the acceptance of Congress, become the Seat of the Government of the United States, and to exercise like Authority over all Places purchased by the Consent of the Legislature of the State in 10 which the Same shall be, for the Erection of Forts, Magazines, Arsenals, dock-Yards, and other needful Buildings; And To make all Laws which shall be necessary and proper for carrying into Execution the foregoing Powers, and all other Powers vested by 15 this Constitution in the Government of the United States, or in any Department or Officer thereof.

SECTION 9. The Migration or Importation of such Persons as any of the States now existing shall think proper to admit, shall not be prohibited by 20 the Congress prior to the Year one thousand eight hundred and eight, but a tax or duty may be imposed on such Importation, not exceeding ten dollars for each Person.

The privilege of the Writ of Habeas Corpus shall 25 not be suspended, unless when in Cases of Rebellion or Invasion the public Safety may require it.

No Bill of Attainder or ex post facto Law shall be passed.

No capitation, or other direct, Tax shall be laid, 30 unless in Proportion to the Census or Enumeration here in before directed to be taken.[5]

No Tax or Duty shall be laid on Articles exported from any State.

5 Changed by the Sixteenth Amendment.

No Preference shall be given by any Regulation of Commerce or Revenue to the Ports of one State over those of another: nor shall Vessels bound to, or from, one State, be obliged to enter, clear, or pay Duties in another.

No Money shall be drawn from the Treasury, but in Consequence of Appropriations made by Law; and a regular Statement and Account of the Receipts and Expenditures of all public Money shall be published from time to time.

No Title of Nobility shall be granted by the United States: And no Person holding any Office of Profit or Trust under them, shall, without the Consent of the Congress, accept of any present, Emolument, Office, or Title, of any kind whatever, from any King, Prince or foreign State.

SECTION 10. No State shall enter into any Treaty, Alliance, or Confederation; grant Letters of Marque and Reprisal; coin Money; emit Bills of Credit; make any Thing but gold and silver Coin a Tender in Payment of Debts; pass any Bill of Attainder, ex post facto Law, or Law impairing the Obligation of Contracts, or grant any Title of Nobility.

No State shall, without the Consent of the Congress, lay any Imposts or Duties on Imports or Exports, except what may be absolutely necessary for executing its inspection Laws: and the net Produce of all Duties and Imposts, laid by any State on Imports or Exports, shall be for the Use of the Treasury of the United States; and all such Laws shall be subject to the Revision and Control of the Congress.

No State shall, without the Consent of Congress, lay any duty of Tonnage, keep Troops, or Ships of War in time of Peace, enter into any Agreement or

1 Compact with another State, or with a foreign Power, or engage in War, unless actually invaded, or in such imminent Danger as will not admit of delay.

Article II.

SECTION 1. The executive Power shall be vested
5 in a President of the United States of America. He shall hold his Office during the Term of four Years, and, together with the Vice-President chosen for the same Term, be elected, as follows:

Each State shall appoint, in such Manner as
10 the Legislature thereof may direct, a Number of Electors, equal to the whole Number of Senators and Representatives to which the State may be entitled in the Congress: but no Senator or Representative, or Person holding an Office of Trust or Profit under the
15 United States, shall be appointed an Elector.

[The Electors shall meet in their respective States, and vote by Ballot for two persons, of whom one at least shall not lie an Inhabitant of the same State with themselves. And they shall make a List of
20 all the Persons voted for, and of the Number of Votes for each; which List they shall sign and certify, and transmit sealed to the Seat of the Government of the United States, directed to the President of the Senate. The President of the Senate shall, in the Presence of
25 the Senate and House of Representatives, open all the Certificates, and the Votes shall then be counted. The Person having the greatest Number of Votes shall be the President, if such Number be a Majority of the whole Number of Electors appointed; and if
30 there be more than one who have such Majority, and have an equal Number of Votes, then the House of Representatives shall immediately choose by

Ballot one of them for President; and if no Person have a Majority, then from the five highest on the List the said House shall in like Manner choose the President. But in choosing the President, the Votes shall be taken by States, the Representation from each State having one Vote; a quorum for this Purpose shall consist of a Member or Members from two-thirds of the States, and a Majority of all the States shall be necessary to a Choice. In every Case, after the Choice of the President, the Person having the greatest Number of Votes of the Electors shall be the Vice President. But if there should remain two or more who have equal Votes, the Senate shall choose from them by Ballot the Vice-President.][6]

The Congress may determine the Time of choosing the Electors, and the Day on which they shall give their Votes; which Day shall be the same throughout the United States.

No person except a natural born Citizen, or a Citizen of the United States, at the time of the Adoption of this Constitution, shall be eligible to the Office of President; neither shall any Person be eligible to that Office who shall not have attained to the Age of thirty-five Years, and been fourteen Years a Resident within the United States.

[In Case of the Removal of the President from Office, or of his Death, Resignation, or Inability to discharge the Powers and Duties of the said Office, the same shall devolve on the Vice President, and the Congress may by Law provide for the Case of Removal, Death, Resignation or Inability, both of the President and Vice President, declaring what Officer shall then act as President, and such Officer shall

6 Changed by the Twelfth Amendment.

1 act accordingly, until the Disability be removed, or a President shall be elected.][7]

The President shall, at stated Times, receive for his Services, a Compensation, which shall neither be
5 increased nor diminished during the Period for which he shall have been elected, and he shall not receive within that Period any other Emolument from the United States, or any of them.

Before he enter on the Execution of his Office,
10 he shall take the following Oath or Affirmation:

"I do solemnly swear (or affirm) that I will faithfully execute the Office of President of the United States, and will to the best of my Ability, preserve, protect and defend the Constitution of the
15 United States."

SECTION 2. The President shall be Commander in Chief of the Army and Navy of the United States, and of the Militia of the several States, when called into the actual Service of the United States; he may
20 require the Opinion, in writing, of the principal Officer in each of the executive Departments, upon any subject relating to the Duties of their respective Offices, and he shall have Power to Grant Reprieves and Pardons for Offenses against the United States,
25 except in Cases of Impeachment.

He shall have Power, by and with the Advice and Consent of the Senate, to make Treaties, provided two thirds of the Senators present concur; and he shall nominate, and by and with the Advice and
30 Consent of the Senate, shall appoint Ambassadors, other public Ministers and Consuls, Judges of the supreme Court, and all other Officers of the United States, whose Appointments are not herein otherwise

---

7 Changed by the Twenty-Fifth Amendment.

provided for, and which shall be established by Law: but the Congress may by Law vest the Appointment of such inferior Officers, as they think proper, in the President alone, in the Courts of Law, or in the Heads of Departments.

The President shall have Power to fill up all Vacancies that may happen during the Recess of the Senate, by granting Commissions which shall expire at the End of their next Session.

SECTION 3. He shall from time to time give to the Congress Information of the State of the Union, and recommend to their Consideration such Measures as he shall judge necessary and expedient; he may, on extraordinary Occasions, convene both Houses, or either of them, and in Case of Disagreement between them, with Respect to the Time of Adjournment, he may adjourn them to such Time as he shall think proper; he shall receive Ambassadors and other public Ministers; he shall take Care that the Laws be faithfully executed, and shall Commission all the Officers of the United States.

SECTION 4. The President, Vice President and all civil Officers of the United States, shall be removed from Office on Impeachment for, and Conviction of, Treason, Bribery, or other high Crimes and Misdemeanors.

Article III.

1 **SECTION 1.** The judicial Power of the United States, shall be vested in one supreme Court, and in such inferior Courts as the Congress may from time to time ordain and establish. The Judges, both of the 5 supreme and inferior Courts, shall hold their Offices during good Behavior, and shall, at stated Times, receive for their Services a Compensation which shall not be diminished during their Continuance in Office.

SECTION 2. The judicial Power shall extend to 10 all Cases, in Law and Equity, arising under this Constitution, the Laws of the United States, and Treaties made, or which shall be made, under their Authority; to all Cases affecting Ambassadors, other public Ministers and Consuls; to all Cases of admiralty 15 and maritime Jurisdiction; to Controversies to which the United States shall be a Party; to Controversies between two or more States; [between a State and Citizens of another State;][8] between Citizens of different States; between Citizens of the same State 20 claiming Lands under Grants of different States, [and between a State, or the Citizens thereof, and foreign States, Citizens or Subjects.][9]

In all Cases affecting Ambassadors, other public Ministers and Consuls, and those in which a State 25 shall be Party, the supreme Court shall have original Jurisdiction. In all the other Cases before mentioned, the supreme Court shall have appellate Jurisdiction, both as to Law and Fact, with such Exceptions, and under such Regulations as the Congress shall make.

30 The Trial of all Crimes, except in Cases of Impeachment, shall be by Jury; and such Trial shall

8 Changed by the Eleventh Amendment.

9 Changed by the Eleventh Amendment.

be held in the State where the said Crimes shall have been committed; but when not committed within any State, the Trial shall be at such Place or Places as the Congress may by Law have directed.

SECTION 3. Treason against the United States, shall consist only in levying War against them, or in adhering to their Enemies, giving them Aid and Comfort. No Person shall be convicted of Treason unless on the Testimony of two Witnesses to the same overt Act, or on Confession in open Court.

The Congress shall have power to declare the Punishment of Treason, but no Attainder of Treason shall work Corruption of Blood, or Forfeiture except during the Life of the Person attainted.

Article IV.

SECTION 1. Full Faith and Credit shall be given in each State to the public Acts, Records, and judicial Proceedings of every other State. And the Congress may by general Laws prescribe the Manner in which such Acts, Records and Proceedings shall be proved, and the Effect thereof.

SECTION 2. The Citizens of each State shall be entitled to all Privileges and Immunities of Citizens in the several States.

A Person charged in any State with Treason, Felony, or other Crime, who shall flee from Justice, and be found in another State, shall on demand of the executive Authority of the State from which he fled, be delivered up, to be removed to the State having Jurisdiction of the Crime.

[No Person held to Service or Labour in one State, under the Laws thereof, escaping into another, shall, in Consequence of any Law or Regulation therein, be discharged from such Service or Labour, But shall be delivered up on Claim of the Party to whom such Service or Labour may be due.][10]

SECTION 3. New States may be admitted by the Congress into this Union; but no new States shall be formed or erected within the Jurisdiction of any other State; nor any State be formed by the Junction of two or more States, or parts of States,without the Consent of the Legislatures of the States concerned as well as of the Congress.

The Congress shall have Power to dispose of and make all needful Rules and Regulations respecting the Territory or other Property belonging to the United States; and nothing in this Constitution shall be so construed as to Prejudice any Claims of the United States, or of any particular State.

SECTION 4. The United States shall guarantee to every State in this Union a Republican Form of Government, and shall protect each of them against Invasion; and on Application of the Legislature, or of the Executive (when the Legislature cannot be convened) against domestic Violence.

Article V.

The Congress, whenever two thirds of both Houses shall deem it necessary, shall propose Amendments to this Constitution, or, on the Application of the Legislatures of two thirds of the several States, shall call a Convention for proposing Amendments, which, in either Case, shall be valid to all Intents and Purposes, as part of this Constitution, when ratified

10 Changed by the Thirteenth Amendment.

by the Legislatures of three fourths of the several States, or by Conventions in three fourths thereof, as the one or the other Mode of Ratification may be proposed by the Congress; Provided that no Amendment which may be made prior to the Year One thousand eight hundred and eight shall in any Manner affect the first and fourth Clauses in the Ninth Section of the first Article; and that no State, without its Consent, shall be deprived of its equal Suffrage in the Senate.

Article VI.

All Debts contracted and Engagements entered into, before the Adoption of this Constitution, shall be as valid against the United States under this Constitution, as under the Confederation.

This Constitution, and the Laws of the United States which shall be made in Pursuance thereof; and all Treaties made, or which shall be made, under the Authority of the United States, shall be the supreme Law of the Land; and the Judges in every State shall be bound thereby, any Thing in the Constitution or Laws of any State to the Contrary notwithstanding.

The Senators and Representatives before mentioned, and the Members of the several State Legislatures, and all executive and judicial Officers, both of the United States and of the several States, shall be bound by Oath or Affirmation, to support this Constitution; but no religious Test shall ever be required as a Qualification to any Office or public Trust under the United States.

Article VII.

1 The Ratification of the Conventions of nine States, shall be sufficient for the Establishment of this Constitution between the States so ratifying the Same.

5 Done in Convention by the Unanimous Consent of the States present the Seventeenth Day of September in the Year of our Lord one thousand seven hundred and Eighty seven and of the Independence of the United States of America the Twelfth. In

10 Witness whereof We have hereunto subscribed our Names.

G. Washington —
President and deputy from Virginia

New Hampshire	John Langdon Nicholas Gilman
Massachusetts	Nathaniel Gorham Rufus King
Connecticut	William Samuel Johnson Roger Sherman
New York	Alexander Hamilton
New Jersey	William Livingston David Brearley William Paterson Jonathan Dayton
Pennsylvania	Benjamin Franklin Thomas Mifflin Robert Morris George Clymer Thomas Fitzsimons Jared Ingersoll James Wilson Gouvernour Morris
Delaware	George Read Gunning Bedford Jr. John Dickinson Richard Bassett Jacob Broom
Maryland	James McHenry Daniel of St Thomas Jenifer Daniel Carroll
Virginia	John Blair James Madison Jr.
North Carolina	William Blount, Richard Dobbs Spaight Hugh Williamson
South Carolina	John Rutledge Charles Cotesworth Pinckney Charles Pinckney Pierce Butler
Georgia	William Few Abraham Baldwin Attest: William Jackson, Secretary

Amendments to the Constitution of the United States of America

The first ten Amendments to the Constitution, the

BILL OF RIGHTS

were ratified effective December 15, 1791.

Amendment 1

1 Congress shall make no law respecting an establishment of religion, or prohibiting the free exercise thereof; or abridging the freedom of speech, or of the press; or the right of the people peaceably
5 to assemble, and to petition the Government for a redress of grievances.

Amendment 2

7 A well regulated Militia, being necessary to the security of a free State, the right of the people to keep and bear Arms, shall not be infringed.

Amendment 3

10 No Soldier shall, in time of peace be quartered in any house, without the consent of the Owner, nor in time of war, but in a manner to be prescribed by law.

Amendment 4

13 The right of the people to be secure in their persons, houses, papers, and effects, against unreasonable

searches and seizures, shall not be violated, and 1
no Warrants shall issue, but upon probable cause,
supported by Oath or affirmation, and particularly
describing the place to be searched, and the persons
or things to be seized. 5

Amendment 5

No person shall be held to answer for a capital, or 6
otherwise infamous crime, unless on a presentment
or indictment of a Grand Jury, except in cases arising
in the land or naval forces, or in the Militia, when
in actual service in time of War or public danger; 10
nor shall any person be subject for the same offense
to be twice put in jeopardy of life or limb; nor shall
be compelled in any criminal case to be a witness
against himself, nor be deprived of life, liberty, or
property, without due process of law; nor shall 15
private property be taken for public use, without just
compensation.

Amendment 6

In all criminal prosecutions, the accused shall enjoy 18
the right to a speedy and public trial, by an impartial
jury of the State and district wherein the crime shall 20
have been committed, which district shall have been
previously ascertained by law, and to be informed
of the nature and cause of the accusation; to be
confronted with the witnesses against him; to have
compulsory process for obtaining witnesses in his 25
favor, and to have the Assistance of Counsel for his
defence.

Amendment 7

1 In Suits at common law, where the value in controversy shall exceed twenty dollars, the right of trial by jury shall be preserved, and no fact tried by a jury, shall be otherwise re-examined in any Court of
5 the United States, than according to the rules of the common law.

Amendment 8

7 Excessive bail shall not be required, nor excessive fines imposed, nor cruel and unusual punishments inflicted.

Amendment 9

10 The enumeration in the Constitution, of certain rights, shall not be construed to deny or disparage others retained by the people.

Amendment 10

13 The powers not delegated to the United States by the Constitution, nor prohibited by it to the States, are reserved to the States respectively, or to the people.

Amendment 11

Ratified February 7, 1795

16 The Judicial power of the United States shall not be construed to extend to any suit in law or equity, commenced or prosecuted against one of the United States by Citizens of another State, or by Citizens or
20 Subjects of any Foreign State.

Amendment 12

Ratified June 15, 1804

The Electors shall meet in their respective states, 1
and vote by ballot for President and Vice-President,
one of whom, at least, shall not be an inhabitant of
the same state with themselves; they shall name in
their ballots the person voted for as President, and in 5
distinct ballots the person voted for as Vice-President,
and they shall make distinct lists of all persons voted
for as President, and of all persons voted for as Vice-
President and of the number of votes for each, which
lists they shall sign and certify, and transmit sealed 10
to the seat of the government of the United States,
directed to the President of the Senate;

The President of the Senate shall, in the presence
of the Senate and House of Representatives, open all
the certificates and the votes shall then be counted; 15

The person having the greatest Number of votes
for President, shall be the President, if such number
be a majority of the whole number of Electors
appointed; and if no person have such majority,
then from the persons having the highest numbers 20
not exceeding three on the list of those voted for
as President, the House of Representatives shall
choose immediately, by ballot, the President. But in
choosing the President, the votes shall be taken by
states, the representation from each state having one 25
vote; a quorum for this purpose shall consist of a
member or members from two-thirds of the states,
and a majority of all the states shall be necessary to
a choice. And if the House of Representatives shall
not choose a President whenever the right of choice 30

1 shall devolve upon them, before the fourth day of March next following, then the Vice-President shall act as President, as in the case of the death or other constitutional disability of the President.

5 The person having the greatest number of votes as Vice-President, shall be the Vice-President, if such number be a majority of the whole number of Electors appointed, and if no person have a majority, then from the two highest numbers on the list, the 10 Senate shall choose the Vice-President; a quorum for the purpose shall consist of two-thirds of the whole number of Senators, and a majority of the whole number shall be necessary to a choice. But no person constitutionally ineligible to the office of 15 President shall be eligible to that of Vice-President of the United States.

Amendment 13

Ratified December 6, 1865

17 1.Neither slavery nor involuntary servitude, except as a punishment for crime whereof the party shall have been duly convicted, shall exist within the United 20 States, or any place subject to their jurisdiction.
2. Congress shall have power to enforce this article by appropriate legislation.

Amendment 14

Ratified July 9, 1868

23 1. All persons born or naturalized in the United States, and subject to the jurisdiction thereof, are citizens of the 25 United States and of the State wherein they reside. No State shall make or enforce any law which shall abridge

the privileges or immunities of citizens of the United States; nor shall any State deprive any person of life, liberty, or property, without due process of law; nor deny to any person within its jurisdiction the equal protection of the laws.

2. Representatives shall be apportioned among the several States according to their respective numbers, counting the whole number of persons in each State, excluding Indians not taxed. But when the right to vote at any election for the choice of electors for President and Vice-President of the United States, Representatives in Congress, the Executive and Judicial officers of a State, or the members of the Legislature thereof, is denied to any of the male inhabitants of such State, being twenty-one years of age, and citizens of the United States, or in any way abridged, except for participation in rebellion, or other crime, the basis of representation therein shall be reduced in the proportion which the number of such male citizens shall bear to the whole number of male citizens twenty-one years of age in such State.

3. No person shall be a Senator or Representative in Congress, or elector of President and Vice-President, or hold any office, civil or military, under the United States, or under any State, who, having previously taken an oath, as a member of Congress, or as an officer of the United States, or as a member of any State legislature, or as an executive or judicial officer of any State, to support the Constitution of the United States, shall have engaged in insurrection or rebellion against the same, or given aid or comfort to the enemies thereof. But Congress may by a vote

of two-thirds of each House, remove such disability.

4. The validity of the public debt of the United States, authorized by law, including debts incurred for payment of pensions and bounties for services in suppressing insurrection or rebellion, shall not be questioned. But neither the United States nor any State shall assume or pay any debt or obligation incurred in aid of insurrection or rebellion against the United States, or any claim for the loss or emancipation of any slave; but all such debts, obligations and claims shall be held illegal and void.

5. The Congress shall have power to enforce, by appropriate legislation, the provisions of this article.

Amendment 15

Ratified February 3, 1870

1. The right of citizens of the United States to vote shall not be denied or abridged by the United States or by any State on account of race, color, or previous condition of servitude.

2. The Congress shall have power to enforce this article by appropriate legislation.

Amendment 16

Ratified February 3, 1913

The Congress shall have power to lay and collect taxes on incomes, from whatever source derived, without apportionment among the several States, and without regard to any census or enumeration.

Amendment 17

Ratified April 8, 1913

The Senate of the United States shall be composed of two Senators from each State, elected by the people thereof, for six years; and each Senator shall have one vote. The electors in each State shall have the qualifications requisite for electors of the most numerous branch of the State legislatures. 1 5

When vacancies happen in the representation of any State in the Senate, the executive authority of such State shall issue writs of election to fill such vacancies: Provided, That the legislature of any State may empower the executive thereof to make temporary appointments until the people fill the vacancies by election as the legislature may direct. 10

This amendment shall not be so construed as to affect the election or term of any Senator chosen before it becomes valid as part of the Constitution. 15

Amendment 18

Ratified January 16, 1919

1. After one year from the ratification of this article the manufacture, sale, or transportation of intoxicating liquors within, the importation thereof into, or the exportation thereof from the United States and all territory subject to the jurisdiction thereof for beverage purposes is hereby prohibited. 17 20

2. The Congress and the several States shall have concurrent power to enforce this article by appropriate legislation. 25

1 3. This article shall be inoperative unless it shall have been ratified as an amendment to the Constitution by the legislatures of the several States, as provided in the Constitution, within seven years from the date of
5 the submission hereof to the States by the Congress.

Amendment 19

Ratified August 18, 1920

6 The right of citizens of the United States to vote shall not be denied or abridged by the United States or by any State on account of sex.

Congress shall have power to enforce this article
10 by appropriate legislation.

Amendment 20

Ratified January 23, 1933

11 1. The terms of the President and Vice President shall end at noon on the 20th day of January, and the terms of Senators and Representatives at noon on the 3d day of January, of the years in which such
15 terms would have ended if this article had not been ratified; and the terms of their successors shall then begin.

2. The Congress shall assemble at least once in every year, and such meeting shall begin at noon on the
20 3d day of January, unless they shall by law appoint a different day.

3. If, at the time fixed for the beginning of the term of the President, the President elect shall have died, the Vice President elect shall become President. If
25 a President shall not have been chosen before the time fixed for the beginning of his term, or if the

President elect shall have failed to qualify, then the Vice President elect shall act as President until a President shall have qualified; and the Congress may by law provide for the case wherein neither a President elect nor a Vice President elect shall have qualified, declaring who shall then act as President, or the manner in which one who is to act shall be selected, and such person shall act accordingly until a President or Vice President shall have qualified.

4. The Congress may by law provide for the case of the death of any of the persons from whom the House of Representatives may choose a President whenever the right of choice shall have devolved upon them, and for the case of the death of any of the persons from whom the Senate may choose a Vice President whenever the right of choice shall have devolved upon them.

5. Sections 1 and 2 shall take effect on the 15th day of October following the ratification of this article.

6. This article shall be inoperative unless it shall have been ratified as an amendment to the Constitution by the legislatures of three-fourths of the several States within seven years from the date of its submission.

Amendment 21

Ratified December 5, 1933

1. The eighteenth article of amendment to the Constitution of the United States is hereby repealed.

2. The transportation or importation into any State, Territory, or possession of the United States for delivery or use therein of intoxicating liquors, in violation of the laws thereof, is hereby prohibited.

1 3. The article shall be inoperative unless it shall have been ratified as an amendment to the Constitution by conventions in the several States, as provided in the Constitution, within seven years from the date of 5 the submission hereof to the States by the Congress.

Amendment 22

Ratified February 27, 1951

6 1. No person shall be elected to the office of the President more than twice, and no person who has held the office of President, or acted as President, for more than two years of a term to which some other person 10 was elected President shall be elected to the office of the President more than once. But this Article shall not apply to any person holding the office of President, when this Article was proposed by the Congress, and shall not prevent any person who may be holding the 15 office of President, or acting as President, during the term within which this Article becomes operative from holding the office of President or acting as President during the remainder of such term.

2. This article shall be inoperative unless it shall have 20 been ratified as an amendment to the Constitution by the legislatures of three-fourths of the several States within seven years from the date of its submission to the States by the Congress.

Amendment 23

Ratified March 29, 1961

24 1. The District constituting the seat of Government of the United States shall appoint in such manner as the Congress may direct:

A number of electors of President and Vice President equal to the whole number of Senators and Representatives in Congress to which the District would be entitled if it were a State, but in no event more than the least populous State; they shall be in addition to those appointed by the States, but they shall be considered, for the purposes of the election of President and Vice President, to be electors appointed by a State; and they shall meet in the District and perform such duties as provided by the twelfth article of amendment.

2. The Congress shall have power to enforce this article by appropriate legislation.

Amendment 24

Ratified January 23, 1964

1. The right of citizens of the United States to vote in any primary or other election for President or Vice President, for electors for President or Vice President, or for Senator or Representative in Congress, shall not be denied or abridged by the United States or any State by reason of failure to pay any poll tax or other tax.

2. The Congress shall have power to enforce this article by appropriate legislation.

Amendment 25

Ratified February 10, 1967

1. In case of the removal of the President from office or of his death or resignation, the Vice President shall become President.

1 2. Whenever there is a vacancy in the office of the Vice President, the President shall nominate a Vice President who shall take office upon confirmation by a majority vote of both Houses of Congress.

5 3. Whenever the President transmits to the President pro tempore of the Senate and the Speaker of the House of Representatives his written declaration that he is unable to discharge the powers and duties of his office, and until he transmits to them a written

10 declaration to the contrary, such powers and duties shall be discharged by the Vice President as Acting President.

4. Whenever the Vice President and a majority of either the principal officers of the executive

15 departments or of such other body as Congress may by law provide, transmit to the President pro tempore of the Senate and the Speaker of the House of Representatives their written declaration that the President is unable to discharge the powers

20 and duties of his office, the Vice President shall immediately assume the powers and duties of the office as Acting President.

Thereafter, when the President transmits to the President pro tempore of the Senate and the

25 Speaker of the House of Representatives his written declaration that no inability exists, he shall resume the powers and duties of his office unless the Vice President and a majority of either the principal officers of the executive department or of such other

30 body as Congress may by law provide, transmit within four days to the President pro tempore of the Senate and the Speaker of the House of Representatives

their written declaration that the President is unable to discharge the powers and duties of his office. Thereupon Congress shall decide the issue, assembling within forty eight hours for that purpose if not in session. If the Congress, within twenty one days after receipt of the latter written declaration, or, if Congress is not in session, within twenty one days after Congress is required to assemble, determines by two thirds vote of both Houses that the President is unable to discharge the powers and duties of his office, the Vice President shall continue to discharge the same as Acting President; otherwise, the President shall resume the powers and duties of his office.

Amendment 26

Ratified July 1, 1971

1. The right of citizens of the United States, who are eighteen years of age or older, to vote shall not be denied or abridged by the United States or by any State on account of age.
2. The Congress shall have power to enforce this article by appropriate legislation.

Amendment 27

Ratified May 7, 1992

No law, varying the compensation for the services of the Senators and Representatives, shall take effect, until an election of Representatives shall have intervened.

GLOSSARY

The following words may have more than one meaning. This list includes definitions that best pertain to the Constitution and the Declaration of Independence. For more detailed definitions of these words as they were understood in the late 1700s, see Noah Webster's "American Dictionary of the English Language," 1828.

ABDICATED – gave up a right, responsibility, or duty

ABSOLVED – set free or released

ACCOMMODATION – the process of adapting or adjusting to someone or something

ACQUIESCE – to agree without protest

ADHERING – being attached as a follower

ADJOURN – to postpone action of a convened legislative body until another time specified

ADMIRALTY AND MARITIME LAW – laws relating to the sea, lakes, and rivers.

ADMIT – to allow

AFFECTED – influenced, aspired to, sought to obtain

AFFIRMATION – declaration, confirmation or ratification that something is true

ALLEGIANCE – loyalty or devotion to a group, person, or cause

AMBASSADOR – an authorized messenger or representative

AMENDMENT – a formal alteration or addition to the United States Constitution.

ANNIHILATION – being destroyed or wiped out completely

APPEAL – to request from some person or authority a decision, reconsideration, judgment; to attract, interest, amuse

APPELLATE – relating to appeals, which are reviews of lower court decisions by a higher court

APPLICATION – a formal request to an authority

APPORTION – give out in portions, divided, allocated, distribute according to a plan; set apart for a special purpose

ARBITRARY – unrestricted, not according to set laws, at the whim of someone else such as a king

ARSENALS – places for making or storing weapons and munitions

ARTICLE – a section or part of a written document

ASCERTAINED – established

ASSEMBLE – to bring together or gather into one place

ASSENT – consent or agreement

ASSUME – to take on, to take over, to take for granted

AT LARGE – free; free roaming; un-captured; in general

ATTAINDER – a law that declares a person an outlaw or criminal without a formal trial; removal of civil rights and property without trial; used to confiscate property of political enemies

ATTAINTED – a French term meaning "touched" by the finger of accusation

BAIL – money given to guarantee a person released from custody will return at an appointed time. If the person fails to return, the money is given up.

BALLOT – a document on which a voter marks a vote

BANDS – things that bind or unite

BENEFICENT – causing good to be done

BILL OF ATTAINDER – a law passed against a person that pronounces him guilty without a trial by jury

BILL OF RIGHTS – the first ten Amendments to the Constitution that were adopted in 1791. They list several human rights the federal government may not disturb.

BILL – a proposed law that is presented for discussion and approval; also, a list of items such as the Bill of Rights

BLESSINGS – favors, mercies, or benefits

BOUNTIES – rewards for performing certain acts for the government such as joining the military

BREACH – violation, disturbance

BRETHREN – associates or peers closely united or connected

BRITAIN, GREAT BRITAIN – before 1707, Britain included England and Wales. In 1707, Scotland joined to create Great Britain. Both terms mean the islands and political union shared by England, Scotland and Wales.

CANDID – transparent; free from prejudice; fair or impartial

CAPITAL – punishable by death

CAPITATION – a poll tax, head tax, uniform amount for each person

CASES – instances; matters to be decided in a court of law

CENSUS – a count of the population

CERTIFICATES – a written and signed document serving as evidence to the truth of facts stated

CERTIFY – make a declaration in writing

CESSION – the act of transferring the title of ownership, such as ceding land to become the seat of government

CHARTER – a document outlining the conditions under which a colony is organized

CHECKS AND BALANCES – "check" means to stop or prevent; "balance" means equal with the others. It's a system set up by the Constitution giving power to the executive, legislative, and judicial branches of government to prevent each other from overreach, and to maintain a "balance" of power.

CHIEF JUSTICE – the senior judge of the Supreme Court

CIVIL – relating to citizens in their ordinary capacity in a community as separate from their role in military, government, or ecclesiastical service

COLONY – a group of people who settle an area away from their homeland, but remain under the political control of their homeland

COMMANDER IN CHIEF – supreme commander of the armed forces

COMMISSION – a written document authorizing a person to perform certain duties; the act of giving a commission

COMMON LAW – that body of ancient and modern rules, Principles, and customs recognized by courts as the law of the land. Not the same as "statutory law," which are laws made by legislatures. (see *People's Law, Ruler's Law*)

COMPACT – contract or treaty

COMPENSATION – amends for service or injury; payment for service

COMPULSORY PROCESS – a legal document ordering a person to appear in court

CONCLUDE – to make a final determination

CONCUR – to agree

CONCURRENCE – agreement

CONCURRENT – existing, occurring, or operating at the same time

CONFEDERATION – a group of independent nations or states joined together. "Confederation" referred to the United States before the Constitution was adopted.

CONGRESS – the legislature of the United States government. The U.S. Congress includes the Senate and House of Representatives. Also, a congress is a meeting of people dealing with issues important to their common good

CONJURED – asked earnestly; brought to mind

CONSANGUINITY – "blood relation," or common ancestors

CONSENT – permission

CONSTITUTING – forming

CONSTITUTION – from the Latin "constitutio," the regulations and orders to establish or to fix what a government is, what it does, and its laws and principles. A written constitution is far more powerful than an oral or assumed understanding. The U.S. Constitution was written at the Constitutional Convention in Philadelphia in 1787 and later ratified by the original thirteen states.

CONSTITUTIONALLY – according to the constitution

CONSTRAINS – forces or compels

CONSTRUED – interpreted or explained; assigned a meaning to something

CONSUL – an official appointed by the government of one country to look after the commercial interests and welfare of its citizens in another country.

CONTROVERSIES – lawsuits

CONVENE – to come together or assemble

CONVENTION – formal meeting of delegates or representatives

CORRESPONDENCE – communication

CORRUPTION OF BLOOD – considering a person guilty of the same crime as a guilty relative, and disqualifying the person from inheriting or retaining the guilty person's properties.

CREDIT – faith and confidence in the ability of others to perform on their promises, such as to repay borrowed money

CROWN – the power of a king

DECENT – fit or suitable

DECLARATION – a public announcement

DECLARE – to state that a person or thing exists in a certain way

DEEM – conclude

DELEGATED POWERS – the 20 powers that are exclusively for the federal government. They are listed in Article I, Section 8.

DEMOCRACY – a government run directly by the people where there are no representatives: "one man, one vote." This works at the lowest levels of government, but after that, representatives are far more efficient in governing the affairs of the nation.

DENOUNCES – proclaims in a threatening or accusing manner

DENY – to refuse to recognize

DEPOSITORY – a place where anything is kept for safekeeping

DEPRIVE – to take away

DESIGN – plan or purpose

DESPOTISM – absolute power or control, tyranny

DEVOLVE – to pass down duties from one person to another at a lower level, such as from president to vice president

DISAVOW – to repudiate or condemn

DISCIPLINE – a level of education or instruction set by Congress

DISPARAGE – to regard as being of little worth

DISPOSE OF – to deal with or settle

DISPOSED – tending or inclined to do or to be something

DISTINCT – separate

DISTRICT – an area of a country or city

DOMESTIC TRANQUILITY – peace at home

DOMESTIC – local, or refers to one's own country

DUE PROCESS OF LAW – the regular administration of justice according to the established rule of laws

DULY – properly, fittingly, at the proper time

DUTY – a payment due to the government such as taxes on imports and exports; that which a person is bound by natural or moral obligation to perform

EFFECT – to produce or cause

EFFECTS – personal belongings

EITHER – one or the other

ELECT – to choose; to select from among others by vote

ELECTOR – a citizen who elects or who has a legal right to vote

ELECTOR – a person who votes at the Electoral College for president and vice president

ELECTORAL COLLEGE – (term not in Constitution) the group of people who elect the president and vice president

ELIGIBLE – qualified, worthy, or allowed

EMANCIPATION – the act of freeing someone from slavery

EMIT – to print or issue and put formally into circulation with authority

EMOLUMENT – compensation for services; salary, wages, fees

ENDOWED – provided with a quality or power

ENDS – the intended purposes

ENFORCE – compel to behave in a certain way

ENGAGEMENTS – obligations by agreement or contract

ENGROSS, ENGROSSED – copied in finished form in large, legible script, as the official copy

ENJOY – to have, possess, and use with satisfaction

ENTANGLING – interlocking in confusion, ensnaring

ENTITLE – to give the right to

ENUMERATION – establishing the number of something

EQUITY – impartial distribution of justice

ESTABLISH – to set up on a permanent basis

EVINCES – to show in a clear manner, to prove beyond reasonable doubt

EX POST FACTO LAW – "after the fact." If a person does something legal and the king later makes it a crime, he can be arrested. Latin, "from a thing done afterward."

EXCISE – a tax on the manufacture, sale, or consumption of various commodities such as liquor, tobacco, etc.

EXCITED – created or caused, as in, "He has excited domestic insurrections"

EXECUTE, EXECUTION – to put into operation

EXECUTIVE BRANCH – one of the three branches of the U.S. government with the purpose of enforcing laws

EXECUTIVE DEPARTMENTS – these are departments in the executive branch such as the Departments of Defense, Commerce and Agriculture. .

EXERCISE – performance of duties

EXPEDIENT – proper under the circumstances

EXPORTATION – the selling and shipping of goods to another state or to a foreign country

FAITH – belief; confidence; trust

FATIGUING – to weaken by harassing

FEDERAL – the central government in league with cooperative states

FELONY – a major crime such as murder, arson, rape, etc.

FIT – convenient

FORFEITURE – losing rights, privileges, property, honor, or office as a penalty or payment for a crime

FORMIDABLE – feared or dreaded

FREE PERSON – someone who is not a slave

FREE – independent and able to think or act without restriction

FULL FAITH AND CREDIT CLAUSE – from Article IV, it means that all states are required to honor the laws, judgments, and public documents of every other state

GENERAL – concerning all or most people

GOVERNMENT – a body that governs; or, the act of direction or controlling

GRAND JURY – a grand jury is a jury that investigates allegations of a crime and issues indictments if it finds there is sufficient evidence to justify a full-fledged trial.

GROUND – foundation; beginning; that which supports anything

HABEAS CORPUS – Latin for "have the body." A writ of habeas corpus is a legal document ordering a person freed from false imprisonment; or, his delivery to a court to decide on the legality of his imprisonment.

HAPPINESS – from Noah Webster, 1828: "The agreeable sensations which spring from the enjoyment of good; that state of a being in which his desires are gratified, by the enjoyment of pleasure without pain; ... indefinite degrees of increase in enjoyment, or gratification of desires. Perfect happiness, or pleasure unalloyed with pain, is not attainable in this life."

HEREIN – in this document

HIGH CRIMES – acts against the public morality that are great but technically are not a felony; or, crimes punishable by death

HIGH SEAS – the open ocean not under the jurisdiction of a country

HITHER – to this place

HOUSE OF REPRESENTATIVES – the "lower" house of Congress in which states are represented based on population. Presently there are 435 members in the House.

HUMBLE – submissive

IMMUNITY, IMMUITIES – protection or exemption from something,

IMMUTABLE – unchanging over time or unable to be changed

IMPEACHMENT – the accusation, charge, or indictment before an appropriate tribunal of misconduct in office; a constitutional "check" the Congress has on the President or other high federal officials. It involves an accusation against that official by the House, and removal from office, or other punishment if found guilty of the impeachment by the Senate.

IMPEL – to drive or urge forward

IMPORTATION – buying of goods from another country

IMPOST – a tax, especially a tax on imported goods

IN GENERAL – relating to or including all members

IN CONSEQUENCE – as a result

INALIENABLE RIGHTS – the natural rights of all men, defined by John Locke as life, liberty, and property; can only be taken away by God. Government is created to protect these rights. Also spelled *un*alienable.

INDICTMENT – a formal written charge against one or more people presented to a court

INESTIMABLE – too valuable or precious to be properly measured or estimated

INEVITABLY – unavoidably

INFAMOUS CRIME – a crime which is punishable by imprisonment or death

INFERIOR OFFICERS – government officials of lower rank than ambassadors, Supreme Court justices, etc.

INOPERATIVE – not working or taking effect

INSTITUTED – set up, established, organized

INSTRUMENT – someone or something used as a means for accomplishing a specific purpose

INSURRECTION – organized opposition to authority

INSURRECTIONS – violent uprisings against authority or government

INTERVENE – to come between disputing people; to intercede

INTOXICATING – making drunk (with alcoholic drinks)

INVESTED – provided with something

INVOLUNTARY SERVITUDE – a slave-like condition. Sometimes British criminals were sold to American colonists to labor for them during the term of their sentence.

JUDICIAL REVIEW – a power the Supreme Court conferred upon itself in the 1803 case of Marbury v. Madison (1803) to review the constitutionality of acts passed by Congress or actions by the president

JUDICIAL BRANCH – one of the three branches of our government assigned to interpret the laws

JUDICIAL – refers to judges, courts, or their functions

JUDICIARY – dealing with courts of law

JUNCTION – act of joining, such as two states to make one

JURISDICTION – the power to govern, to make, declare or apply the law; the territory within which power can be exercised

JUST – honest; conforming to moral and proper principles of social conduct

JUSTICE – from Noah Webster, 1828: "The virtue which consists in giving to every one what is his due; practical conformity to the laws and principles of rectitude in the dealings of men with each other."

KINDRED – related by blood

LAID – imposed as a burden or penalty

LAW OF NATIONS – from Noah Webster, 1828: "The rules that regulate the mutual intercourse of nations or states. These rules depend on natural law, or the principles of justice which spring from the social state..."

LAW – rules established by governments for regulating people's actions

LAWS OF NATURE – from Noah Webster, 1828: "a rule of conduct arising out of the natural relations of human beings established by the Creator, and existing prior to any positive precept. Thus it is a law of nature, that one man should not injure another, and murder and fraud would be crimes, independent of any prohibition from a supreme power."

LAY – to set or impose (to lay and collect taxes)

LEGISLATIVE – referring to the power to make laws

LEGISLATURE – people who make or amend or repeal laws

LETTERS OF MARQUE AND REPRISAL – from Noah Webster, 1828: "a commission granted by a supreme authority of a state to a subject, empowering him to pass the frontiers [marque] that is, enter an enemy's territories and capture the goods and persons of the enemy, in return for goods and persons taken by him." See *Reprisal.*

LEVYING – collecting money for public use by tax; collecting soldiers for military or other public service by enlistment

LIBERTY – from Noah Webster, 1828: "Freedom from restraint, in a general sense, and applicable to the body, or to the will or mind; the power to act as one thinks fit, without any restraint or control, except from the laws of nature; freedom of a nation or state from all unjust abridgment of its rights and independence by another nation."

LIFE – the condition in which a human being's natural functions and motions are performed. In mankind, that state of being in which the spirit, intellect, and body are united we identify as life.

MAGAZINES – places of storage or military supply depots

MAGNANIMITY – the quality of being noble and generous in one's conduct and rising above pettiness or meanness

MAJORITY – more than half; the main part

MANLY – brave

MEASURES – inches, feet, yards, etc.; also, actions to be taken

MERCENARIES – hired soldiers

MILITIA – body of soldiers organized from the civilian population in times of emergencies

MISCONSTRUCTION – mistaking the true meaning

MISDEMEANORS – offenses less serious than crimes

MOCK – to imitate or mimic in contempt or derision; to deride

MODE – manner; method

NATIVE – conferred by birth, produced by nature

NATURALIZATION – the granting to a person of foreign birth the rights of citizenship in a new country

NATURALIZE – to make into a citizen

NATURAL LAW – a law that is discoverable by reason, based on right reason, of universal application, and is unchanging and everlasting. Natural Law brings about cooperative harmony and is basic in its principles; it is comprehensible to the human mind and protects human rights; it guides the creation of all moral laws.

NAY – a "no" vote

NET – to produce a clear profit after all deductions have been made

NOMINATE – to propose as a candidate for some honor

NOTWITHSTANDING – without being affected by the particular factor mentioned

OATH – a formal declaration with an appeal to God for the truth of what is being declared

OBJECT – aim or goal

OFFICE – a particular duty or employment

OFFICERS – persons commissioned or authorized to perform a public duty.

OPERATIVE – producing a desired effect

ORDAIN – officially order

ORIGINAL JURISDICTION – the authority to try a case from its beginning

OTHER OFFICERS – people appointed to positions of responsibility in the government

OTHER PUBLIC MINISTERS – government officials sent to represent their own government in another country and ranking below an ambassador

OVERT ACT – the act of committing a crime that is open to view

PARALLELED – equaled

PARDON – lessening or setting aside the punishment for a crime

PEACE – a state of quiet or tranquility; freedom from disturbance or agitation; freedom from war or internal commotion; that quiet, order and security which is guaranteed by the laws

PEOPLE – the group of people who make up a nation

PEOPLE'S LAW – natural law; self-rule, self-government: all decisions and selection of leaders are done with consent of the people, laws must comply with natural law, power is dispersed among the people, resolving problems happens on local level, every adult has a voice and a vote, rights are unalienable, government has no more rights than the people themselves have, government's rights are delegated rights

PERFIDY – treachery

PETITIONED – made a formal request

POLITICAL – relating to government or public affairs

POLL TAX – a tax of a fixed amount per person and payable before they may vote ("poll" means a person's head)

POST ROADS – roads over which mail is carried

POSTERITY – all of a person's descendants; all future generations or future mankind

POWERS – rights and authorities; influential countries. Powers reserved to the states are identified in the Tenth Amendment.

PREJUDICE – to hurt, damage, or dismiss

PRESCRIBE – to lay down rules; to order or direct

PRESENTMENT – a report made by a grand jury of an offense that the grand jury observed or learned during their investigations

PRESIDENT PRO TEMPORE – the senior member of the majority party in the Senate who serves as the president of the Senate when the Vice President is absent

PRESIDENT – the person who holds the office of head of state of the United States government

PRIVILEGE, PRIVILEGED – enjoying a peculiar right, permission, or immunity

PRO TEMPORE – temporary, for the time being

PROBABLE CAUSE – a valid reason in presuming someone is guilty of some illegal act

PRODUCE – yield or product, as in "the net Produce of all Duties and Imposts"

PROHIBIT – to command against

PROVIDE – to make available for use; to make adequate preparation; to enable or allow

PROVIDED – "provided" is used in legal documents to introduce a condition or requirement

PROVIDENCE – God or the protective care of nature as a spiritual power

PRUDENCE – good judgment

PUBLIC DOMAIN – the lands held by the state or the federal government

PUBLIC – in open view

PUBLISH – to formally announce

PURSUANCE – the carrying out of something in the way that is expected or required

QUARTERING – lodging

QUORUM – the minimum number of members of a group required to be present to make the actions of that assembly valid

RATIFICATION – making valid by formally confirming

RATIFIED – formally approved and invested with legal authority

RATIFY – to give formal approval to something

RECESS – suspension of business

RECTITUDE – correctness of behavior

REDRESS – the setting right of what is wrong; satisfaction or compensation for a wrong or injury

RENDER – to cause to be; to make, perform, furnish, provide, exhibit

REPRESENTATIVE – a person who acts on behalf of the voters or a community in a legislative body

REPRIEVES – postponements of punishments

REPRISAL – from Noah Webster, 1828: to capture "the goods and persons of the enemy, in return for goods and persons taken by him." See *Letters of Marque and Reprisal.*

REPUBLIC, REPUBLICAN – the type of government in which voters elect representatives to make the laws for the country.

REQUISITE – required or necessary for relief or supply

RESERVING – retaining, keeping back, saving for another

RESIGNATION – the act of giving up an office or position

RESOLUTION – formal expression of opinion or intention by a legislature

RESPECT – that positive view or honor in which we hold the good qualities of others; to give regard, good will, favor

RESPECTING – regarding, in view of, considering

RESPECTIVELY – separately or individually

RETURNS – reports on the count of votes at polling places

RHODE ISLAND AND PROVIDENCE PLANTATIONS – the name of four early settlements in today's Rhode Island

RIGHT – from Noah Webster, 1828: "Conformity to the will of God or to his law, the perfect standard of truth and justice"; a power, privilege, moral or legal claim which correctly belongs to a person by law, by nature, or by tradition; to correct a wrong; to restore to normal or correct condition

RULER'S LAW – rule by the king where all power and rights are in the king, for example: people are not equal, all property is ruler's, power is from top down, no unalienable rights, ruled by whim of the ruler, no fixed rule of law, ruler issues edicts that are law, freedom never considered a solution

SEAT – site of the government; place of official capacity

SECURE – make certain; not exposed to danger, in safe custody

SECURITIES – investments that are easily bought or sold

SEDITION – attempt to overthrow or interrupt a government

SELF-EVIDENT – plain or obvious in itself without more proof

SENATE – one of the two houses of Congress (the "upper" house) with two representatives from each state. Presently there are 100 senators.

SERVITUDE – slavery or bondage to an owner or master

SEVERAL – individual, separate, or distinct

SITTING – present to perform its business

SOVEREIGN – independent, holding all power and authority

SPEAKER OF THE HOUSE – the presiding officer of the U.S. House of Representatives

SPEAKER – the officer presiding over a lawmaking body, such as the House of Representatives

STANDING – status, permanently in existence

STATES' RIGHTS – all rights not delegated to the federal government or denied to the states

STATION – position or rank

STRICT INTERPRETATION – interpreting the Constitution based on its literal words, meaning, and intention

SUBSCRIBED – attested by signing at the end of a document

SUBSTANCE – means of living; also the matter of which things consist

SUCCESSOR – that which comes next; a person who follows next in order

SUFFERABLE – able to be tolerated

SUFFERANCE – tolerating, enduring patiently

SUFFRAGE – the right to vote

SUPERSEDE – to take the place or move into the position of

SUPPRESS – to stop or put to an end by force or authority

TENURE – the period or term for holding an office

TERRITORY – a region controlled by the government

THEREBY – by or through that

THEREFORE – for that reason

THEREIN – in that place

THEREOF – of that

TRAIN – a series or procession of things or acts

TRANQUILITY – calmness

TRANSIENT – not lasting, of short duration

TRIBUNALS – courts

TRY – examine according to law; to try in court

TYRANNY – cruel, oppressive, or unjust government

UNALIENABLE – not capable of being sold, separated, or taken. See *Inalienable.*

UNCONSTITUTIONAL – an act that violates the Constitution

UNDISTINGUISHED – indifferent; not discriminating; not selective; as in "whose known rule of warfare, is undistinguished destruction of all ages, sexes and conditions" (from the Declaration of Independence)

UNION – the group of independent states joined together

UNWARRANTABLE – unjustifiable

USURPATION – the wrongful taking of power or a right

VALIDITY – being legitimate and rigorous

VEST, VESTED – to place or to have placed in the control of a person or group

VETO – to reject or refuse to sign a bill from Congress

VIOLATION – disregarding an agreement or a right

VIZ. – abbreviation of the Latin word "videlicet" meaning "that is to say"

WANTING – lacking

WEIGHTS – ounces, pounds, tonnage, etc.

WELFARE – well-being, prosperity and happiness; national well-being promoted within restrictions permitted by the Constitution.

WHATSOEVER – of any kind

WORKS – actions, deeds, achievements

WRIT OF HABEAS CORPUS – see *habeas corpus*

WRIT – a formal legal document ordering some action

WRITS OF ELECTION – formal written documents ordering elections

YEA – a "yes" vote

Endnotes

INTRODUCTION

Note: This book is meant to be a short introduction, not an exhaustive examination of the founding documents. The basic information is found in any encyclopedia or history textbook. For the reader's convenience, please see cited references below for source materials and additional resources.

Pg. v

Jefferson Quote about education being the best "corrective of abuses of constitutional powers"—Jefferson letter to William Charles Jarvis, September 28, 1820, see the Papers of Thomas Jefferson, National Archives.

Pg. 1

Word count: 4,379 words in the Constitution does not include the signatures.

Pg. 3-6

The Rule of Law, People's Law and Ruler's Law: for more details, quotes by the Framers and ancient philosophers, see W. Cleon Skousen, The Making of America, "Discovery of the Ancient Principles,"

Seven Pillars of Tyranny: There are seven common patterns of control and manipulation present in all systems of tyranny and socialism. For an exhaustive list of examples in history, see Paul B. Skousen, The Naked Socialist.

THE DECLARATION OF INDEPENDENCE

Pg. 8

Word Count: The actual number of words in the Declaration, without the signers, was determined by Harvard University (Harvard.edu) to be 1,337 including the title and date. With the names of the signers included, it's 1,458.

Pg. 11-13

The Eight Ancient Principles given in the first two paragraphs of the Declaration are summaries of principles the Framers discussed in greater depth in their many writings. The main principles Jefferson wove into the Declaration were drawn from many sources including:

John Locke (1632-1704), "Essay Concerning Human Understanding"; on unalienable rights, see "Of Civil Government, Book Two," XI:136n; Locke on life, liberty and property, see "Of Civil Government, Book Two," II:11, III:56, V: 25, 55; XVIII:200; Locke on duty of government to protect rights, see "Of Civil Government, Book Two"; Locke on citizens' right to delegate to government the right to self defense and self government, see "Second Treatise of Government," 1689.

Sir William Blackstone (1723-1780), "Commentaries on the Laws of England," quoted by Hall, "Christian History of the Constitution, pp. 140-146; see also Duncan Kennedy, "Structure of Blackstone's Commentaries," p. 250, where Blackstone says judges were not a source of law, and saw the legislature as superior to the judicial for that reason.

Montesquieu (1689-1755) writing "The Spirit of Laws" said all law has its source in God, and man-made laws must conform to God's law (See Werner Stark, "Montesquieu, Pioneer of the Sociology of Knowledge," Toronto, University of Toronto Press, 1961, pp. 14-16); Montesquieu writing in "The Spirit of Laws" said all men possess the same qualities such as free agents, to choose, see Werner Stark, "Montesquieu, Pioneer of the Sociology of Knowledge," Toronto, University of Toronto Press, 1961, pp. 14-16.

Sir Edward Coke (1552-1634), opponent of the illegal exercise of governmental authority, "Institutes of the Laws of England."

Hugo Grotius (1583-1645) discusses the existence, attributes and providence of God, see "Grotius' Universe: Divine Law and a Quest for Harmony" by

William Vasilio Sotirovich, New York: Vantage Press, 1978, p. 27; Grotius on nature's laws superior to man's laws, see "Commentary on the Law of Prize and Booty," Oxford: Clarendon Press, 1950, p. 8, quoted by Sotirovich, "Grotius' Universe," p. 46.

James Wilson (1742-1798) wrote that all law comes from God, see James DeWitt Andres "Works of Wilson," (Chicago, 1896), 1:91-93;

Algernon Sidney (1623-1683), on governments permitted to exist and arguing against absolute monarchy, opposing divine right of kings, reasoning that the individual has the right to choose his own form of government and to abolish it if it becomes corrupt, and that obedience to corrupt government not required, see "Discourse Concerning Government"

Emmerich de Vattel (1714-1767), "The Law of Nations," pp. 293-296, 1758, discusses each nation has the liberty to govern itself as it pleases.

John Milton (1608-1674) discusses people's rightful control over their government, to form, change and abolish it, see "Tenure of Kings and Magistrates," see Encyclopedia Britannica, 1896, Milton, John.

The King James Bible (1611), with an emphasis on Exodus, Leviticus, Numbers, Deuteronomy, Matthew, Mark.

For an interesting examination of the various sources and influences that the available books and papers had on the Framers' knowledge of individual rights and good government, see John Eidsmoe, "Christianity and the Constitution, The Faith of Our Founding Fathers," Baker Book house, Grand Rapids, Michigan, 1987, where Eidsmoe lists the thinkers, books and writings most frequently cited by the Framers in their discourses and speeches.

Pg. 17-19

The Rule of Law, People's Law and Ruler's Law, used with permission from W. Cleon Skousen, The Making of America, "Discovery of the Ancient Principles,"

Seven Pillars of Tyranny: There are seven common patterns present in all systems of tyranny and socialism. For examples in history, see Paul B. Skousen, The Naked Socialist, pp. 5-11, 28-173.

P. 26

Historical Basics of the Declaration: The draft paper was not hemp, see the Thomas Jefferson Foundation discussion at www.monticello.org.

Word Count: The actual number of words in the Declaration, without the signers, was determined by Harvard University (Harvard.edu) to be 1,337 including the title and date. With the names of the signers included, it's 1,458.

Pg. 27

Jefferson said the Declaration's creation was "not to find out new principles, or new arguments, never before thought of, not merely to say things which had never been said before, but to place before mankind the common sense of the subject in terms so plain and firm as to command their assent, and to justify ourselves in the independent stand we are compelled to take. Neither aiming at originality of principle or sentiment, nor yet copied from any particular and previous writing, it was intended to be an expression of the American mind, and to give to that expression the proper tone and spirit called for by the occasion" Letter to Henry Lee, May 8, 1826.

Pg. 37

Deleted Passage on Slavery. This originally appeared as Charge #27, but was deleted before final passage, an act Jefferson blamed on pro-slavery factions from southern states. See The Writings of Thomas Jefferson, Taylor & Maury, 1853-1854).

"He has waged cruel war against human nature itself, violating its most sacred rights of life and liberty in the persons of a distant people who never offended him, captivating & carrying them into slavery in another hemisphere or to incur miserable death in their transportation thither. This piratical warfare, the opprobrium of infidel powers, is the warfare of the Christian King of Great Britain. Determined to keep open a market where Men should be bought & sold, he has prostituted his negative for suppressing every legislative attempt to prohibit or restrain this execrable commerce. And that this assemblage of horrors might want no fact of distinguished die, he is now exciting those very people to rise in arms among us, and to purchase that liberty of which he has deprived them, by murdering the people on whom he has obtruded them: thus paying off former crimes committed again the Liberties of one people, with crimes which he urges them to commit against the lives of another."

THE CONSTITUTION

Pg. 53

LEJ SASR: Article VI also includes important economic declarations about war debt repayment, and asks for a personal oath to support the new Constitution. The author's sister, Sharon Skousen Krey, suggested making the second "S" a dollar sign "$" to bring to mind war debts, written as: LEJ SA$R.

Pg. 61

Bill of Rights: See Alfred H. Kelly and Winfred A Harbison, The American Constitution, Its Origins and Development, "The Bill of Rights" pp 174-177

20 Powers: Government is granted only 20 powers, see Article 1.8.

Alexander Hamilton: An example of reasons to oppose a list of rights, see The Federalist Papers, No. 84.

Almost 300 Rights: For a list, history, and explanation of 286 constitutional rights protected by the Constitution, see W. Cleon Skousen, The Making of America.

Pg. 79

Examples of controversial judicial rulings that some claim are in violation of Amendments IX and X: Legal abortion (Roe v. Wade), same-sex marriage (Obergefell v. Hodges), Affordable Care Act "Obamacare" (NFIB v. Sebelius).

Pg. 89-91

Abolishing the enemies of freedom using the Constitution is presented in greater detail in The Naked Socialist, Paul B. Skousen, pp. 194-244.

Diluting power vertically and horizontally: Polybius (204-122 BC) first suggested sharing political power among many to prevent tyrants from taking over. Montesquieu suggested separation of powers. Jefferson called for political power to be divided among the many. For more information and citations see Skousen, The Naked Socialist, pp. 181-191.

Leveling: Sam Adams, "The Utopian schemes of leveling and a community of goods, are as visionary and impractical as those ideas which vest all property in the crown." See Skousen, The Naked Socialist, pp. 214-217.

Pg. 99

"If you don't ask the questions you'll never hear the answers," wise council given to the author by his father to spark interest in the vast resources available to discover in-depth knowledge about history, science, principles, and values.

Pg. 102

Prepare for war: Benjamin Franklin: "The way to secure peace is to be prepared for war..." Smyth, The writings of Benjamin Franklin, 2:352

George Washington: "To be prepared for war is one of the effectual means of preserving peace." Fitzpatrick, The Writings of George Washington, 30:491, 31:402.

Pg. 103

General Welfare and Specific Welfare: The hotly debated power to spend was resolved with the 1936 Butler Case where Congress was given power to spend money on "specific welfare." See Skousen, Making of America, pp. 387-392.

"Wisest constitution" Sam Adams quote, see The Life and Public Service of Samuel Adams, Volume 1 (1865), by William Vincent Wells.

Pg. 115

Regulatory Agencies: Regulation over industries started with the Interstate Commerce Commission established by Congress in 1887. This prototype served as the model by which other regulatory agencies were formed. They combine the government's two functions of legislative and judicial powers to pass and enforce new regulatory laws. The President may appoint the leaders of agencies.

Pg. 116

Check on the Supreme Court: Thomas Jefferson's Kentucky Resolution dealt with nullification of federal laws that a state deemed unconstitutional, citing the Tenth Amendment as their authority. (See Kentucky Resolutions of 1798).

Thomas Jefferson—Constitution vulnerable to change by Judiciary: "The constitution, on this hypothesis, is a mere thing of wax in the hands of the judiciary, which they may twist and shape into any form they please." (Letter to Judge Spencer Roane, September 6, 1819

Thomas Jefferson indirectly suggested justices should be elected: "You seem to consider the judges the ultimate arbiters of all constitutional questions; a very dangerous doctrine indeed, and one which would place us under the despotism of an oligarchy. Our judges ... and their power [are] the more dangerous as they are in office for life, and are not responsible, as the other functionaries are, to the elective control." (Letter to Mr. Jarvis, Sept, 1820).

Pg. 122

James Madison, "improve and perpetuate": "They accomplished a revolution which has no parallel in the annals of human society. They reared the fabrics of governments which have no model on the face of the globe. They formed the design of a great Confederacy, which it is incumbent on their successors to improve and perpetuate. If their works betray imperfections, we wonder at the fewness of them." The Federalist Papers #14, November 30, 1787.

Pg. 128

Historical Basics, Word Count Constitution: There are dozens of ways to count the words in the Constitution. For our purposes, we start with "We the People" and end with the final word of Article VII, ". . . so ratifying the Same." That count is 4,379 words. Add the correction paragraph, George Washington's sign off, and the signers' names and states and the total count is 4,609 according to the transcript available at the National Archives Catalog.

Pg. 134

286 Rights: For the list, history, and explanation of the 286 constitutional rights protected by the Constitution, see Skousen, The Making of America.

Pg. 135

Every five lines in the Constitution and Declaration are numbered. This helps make fast references to specific locations in the texts.

DEDICATION

This book is fondly dedicated to my father, W. Cleon Skousen (1913-2006), whose lifetime of research, writing, speaking and teaching about the Constitution inspired an entire generation of Americans. With works such as *The Naked Communist, The 5000 Year Leap*, and *The Making of America*, his readers have influenced positive, principle-based political change on numerous local, state and federal levels. He had that wonderful gift of distilling the complex into the simple, whereby he brought many difficult concepts to the understanding and appreciation of freedom-seeking people everywhere. Much of the research for this book is drawn from my father's files, books and speeches, with great respect, love and admiration.

Answers

Declaration of Independence, pages 22-25

1. July 4, 1776
2. Britain
3. Separate and Equal Station
4. Human Rights
5. Laws of Nature and Nature's God
6. Self-evident: obvious, clear, plain
7. Unalienable: unable to be taken away
8. To secure rights
9. Consent from the people
10. Yes; No
11. Throw off old government, provide new guards
12. 3; 1; 1
13. 9; consent; laws
14. War
15. Indian Savages (American Indians)
16. Redress
17. No
18. Unfit
19. Common kindred; No
20. Levy war; conclude peace; contract alliances; establish commerce; all other acts
21. God
22. Lives, fortunes, sacred honor

Constitution, pages 56-58

1. 7
2. Article I
3. Article VII
4. Article I
5. V, VI, VII
6. Section
7. Article, Section, Clause
8. Lej Sasr
9. In brackets
10. Legislative
11. Executive
12. Judicial
13. Article II
14. Article IV
15 Article V
16. Article VII
17. Opinion (Hint: Framers wanted state's interests represented in D.C. by someone under *regular* scrutiny by legislature)
18. The people; No; No; Education

Bill of Rights, pages 87-88

1 10
2. 189
3. 10
4. Fifth Amendment (108 words; 6th is 81 words)
5. Eighth Amendment (16 words)
6. Your choice
7. Tenth Amendment
8. Eighth Amendment
9. Fifth Amendment (due process clause)
10. First Amendment
11. To cause a riot; to violate other people's rights; national security
12. Fifth Amendment
13. Libel, hearsay, inciting insurrection; revealing national secrets, endangering lives

Preamble, pages 101-103

1. We the People
2. 6
3. Form a more perfect Union, establish justice, insure domestic tranquility, provide for the common defense, promote general welfare, secure blessings of liberty
4. The states
5. Vigilante mobs hanging people without a trial; rich people buying their way out of a trial; favoritism and protectionism by high political figures for friends; etc.
6. a. Military, national guard, FBI, federal court system, stability in national government
   b. Police, fire department, state militia, stability in local government
7. a.&b.: Islamic terrorists; Russia; North Korea; ISIS/ISIL; drug lords, identity thieves, etc.
   c.&d.: inner-city gangs; drug lords; organized crime; felons; traitors; etc.
8. a.&b.: any expenditures that do not directly benefit the entire nation such as building projects in one state, federal loans to some that are not available to others. Food Stamps and Medicaid are "specific welfare" expenses, etc.
9. Opinion question

Article I, pages 107-112

Section 1

1. Congress, the Legislative Branch
2. House; Senate

Section 2

1. 2 years
2. 25 years old
3. House of Representatives

Section 3

1. 6 years
2. 30 years old
3. 1/3
4. Senate
5. Removal from office

Section 4

1. Yes

Section 5

1. Yes
2. Permission of the other

Section 6

1. No
2. No

Section 7

1. House of Representatives
2. Two thirds

Section 8

1. Power to tax
2. Power to spend
3. Power to borrow
4. Regulate commerce
5. Make rules for citizenship, immigration
6. Make bankruptcy laws
7. Coin money, regulate its value
8. Fix standard weights and measurements
9. Punish counterfeiters
10. Establish Post Offices and Postal Roads
11. Protect copyrights and patents
12. Establish courts below the Supreme Court
13. Punish international criminals
14. Declare War
15. Raise and finance the military
16. Makes rules of engagement by American military
17. Call up State militias
18. Administer Washington DC, the seat of government
19. Administer federal lands
20. Make all laws necessary to execute these powers

Section 9

1. Congress can't stop slave importation
2. Habeas Corpus can't be suspended. If a person is thrown in jail his lawyer may give the judge a demand (writ) to see his client to decide if there is enough reason to keep him in jail. "Writ" means "a court order." "Habeas" means "to have." "Corpus" means "the body." Together it means "you have the person" and with the writ, it means, "you have the person, produce him for legal examination."
3. No new laws that suddenly make people guilty for past acts
4. No capitation or direct taxes
5. No tax or duty on states' exports
6. Federal regulation will not show preference of one state over another
7. No money taken from treasury without Congress's approval
8. No aristocratic or privileged classes are allowed in America

Section 10

Clause 1

1. No Treaties
2. No Grant Letters
3. No Coining Money
4. No Bills of Credit
5. No Gold/Silver Coins
6. No Bill of Attainder
7. No Ex Post Facto laws
8. No laws against Legal Agreements
9. No Titles of Nobility

Clause 2

1. No

Clause 3

1. No; if invaded or in imminent danger

Article II, pages 113-114

Section 1

1. 4 years
2. Executive Branch, President
3. Same number as that State's representatives and senators
4. Congress
5. No

Section 2

1. Military; state militias
2. No

Section 3

1. Yes
2. No

Section 4

1. Treason, Bribery, High Crimes and Misdemeanors

Article III, pages 117-118

Section 1

1. Congress's
2. For Life

Section 2

1. Yes
2. Laws and treaties, U.S. representatives, military matters, between states, between citizens of different states, between U.S. representatives and states, etc.
3. Impeachment
4. So that witnesses and family can attend the proceedings with the least amount of expense and inconvenience.

Section 3

1. Waging war against the U.S.; giving aid and comfort to enemies of the U.S.
2. 2
3. Congress

Article IV, pages 119-121

Section 1

1. Yes
2. Driver's license, accredited college degrees, owner of property, adoption, state taxes owed/paid, indebtedness, insurance coverage, bank loans, checking accounts, savings, etc.

Section 2

1. Privilege
2. No

Section 3

1. Yes
2. No
3. No
4. Congress

Section 4

1. Republican (representative)
2. People have representatives

Article V, pages 122-123

Clause 1

1. Yes
2. Two Thirds
3. Three fourths
4. Yes
5. Two thirds
6. No, they must still be ratified by the legislatures of three fourths of the states
7. Three fourths

Article VI, pages 124-125

1. All
2. The U.S. Constitution
3. Oath or Affirmation
4. No

Article VII, page 127

1. 9
2. September 17, 1787

ABOUT THE AUTHOR

Paul B. Skousen is an investigative journalist, writer, and teacher. He received his MA from Georgetown University in National Security Studies. In the 1980s he was a CIA military analyst and intelligence officer in the Situation Room at the White House. He has published several books on politics and history, and is a professor of communications and journalism.

Made in the USA
Coppell, TX
06 November 2021